Wherever Love May Lead

YOUR PLACE IN GOD'S PLAN

Catherine Duerr

CONCORDIA PUBLISHING HOUSE · SAINT LOUIS

Concordia
Publishing House

Founded in 1869 as the publishing arm of The Lutheran
Church—Missouri Synod, Concordia Publishing House gives
all glory to God for the blessing of 150 years of opportunities
to provide resources that are faithful to the Holy Scriptures
and the Lutheran Confessions.

Published by Concordia Publishing House
3558 S. Jefferson Ave., St. Louis, MO 63118–3968
1-800-325-3040 • cph.org

Copyright © 2019 Catherine Duerr

1 2 3 4 5 6 7 8 9 10   28 27 26 25 24 23 22 21 20 19

Dedicated to Tommy, Valarie, Tony, Josh, and Mayo

From you, I learned how the mission
field can be in my own home.

May God bless you all wherever He takes you.

Table of Contents

INTRODUCTION

HOW TO USE THIS BOOK

Have you ever wondered if you are on the path God wants you to be on? Have you pondered your purpose in life? In *Wherever Love May Lead: Your Place in God's Plan,* we will explore various vocations and how God is calling us wherever we are. We will see people in the Bible and in our current world living out their vocations, and we'll look at our own lives and search out how God calls us. It is my prayer that you will be encouraged in how God is already using you and challenged in new ways that He wants to love people through you. I want to be clear that you are not expected to engage in every vocation or in the same manner as the people presented here. These examples are meant to inspire and encourage, not make you feel guilty.

How This Study Is Structured

Wherever Love May Lead includes daily study that individuals can do either for their own personal learning or in preparation for a group study (see "Suggestions for Small Groups" on the next page).

Each day looks at the Bible to see where and how God worked through His people. You will read an anecdote to see how ordinary people of today are living out their vocations and are being used for God's plan. Then you are given a few questions to help you explore areas that God is calling you to.

Each week suggests a memory verse that captures the general theme for that week. I encourage you to learn this verse and keep it at the fore throughout the week.

Finally, I am going to ask you to write in your journal. This takes time, but I encourage you to give it a try for at least a week; you may find that journaling is one of the biggest blessings of the whole study. There is a journal prompt for every lesson, but if you feel inspired to write about something else, by all means pursue that. If you want to spend your journal time writing a prayer, that would be a wonderful use of this time. The goal of the study and the journal prompts is to get you to explore how God is calling you. But the prompts are just starting points; be open to deviating from them. You may want to get a blank book or start a document on your computer to use as a journal so you will have all forty in one place.

Suggestions for Small Groups

1. Complete the daily lessons on your own; then be ready to share your already prepared answers with the group.

2. When you meet, open with prayer for your study and for one another.

3. Go over your answers together. Answers that might give insight and further your study are provided in the Leader's Guide in the back of this book.

4. Don't feel the need to read all of your journal entries, but be prepared to share some personal insights that you gained from the study or the journal.

WEEK 1

Called by God

God has called you to be a missionary. Now, don't be alarmed; you don't have to quit school or your job, sell everything, and move to Africa. He asks only a few people to go abroad. And as far as selling everything, you may need some of those possessions in your ministry right where you are. So, if you are not going to Africa, then where *is* your mission field? That is what we are going to explore in this book. God calls His people in all areas and in every place.

Memory Verse: "And who knows whether you have not come to the kingdom for such a time as this?" Esther 4:14b

DAY 1

VOCATION

Read 2 Samuel 5.

"What do you do?" the lab tech asked as we waited for the equipment to charge. What do I *do*? He probably wanted a one-word answer just to make small talk. He was asking what my job was—specifically, what I am paid to do. But what I do can't be reduced to one word.

I had been asked this question before, so I was ready with a response that I thought would satisfy his question: "I am a stay-at-home mom."

Usually that answer ends conversations as if there is nothing more to say. But the opposite is true; there is so much more to my job than a one-sentence answer. What I wanted to say to the lab tech was "I am so much more than what that must sound like to you. First, I am a wife. And yes, I am a mom. I have pictures; let me tell you how awesome my children are. I could talk for hours about them. Mark, Nick, and Angela are the three I gave birth to. There were two before them who never made it to being born; they are in heaven now. I'm also a foster mom. I have had four foster children of varying ages and for varying lengths of time. And I am a guardian to Tony. He has pretty much lived with us since his birth, and Steve and I are privileged to raise him. I am a daughter, sister, aunt, and friend. I am a child of the Most High God. I am a church member, bell ringer, substitute teacher, and Bible study participant. I used to be an elementary schoolteacher. Currently I am an author. This variety in my life gives me character. All of these things are part of my God-ordained vocations."

Vocation. Isn't that a fancy word for "real job"? Not exactly. The word comes from a Latin word meaning "calling." Our vocation is our calling from God. It can be a calling to full-time church work. But it doesn't have to be. It can be a calling to a career, which is how we most often hear the word used. But vocation doesn't have to be a paid position. It is anything God has called us to do. And He gives us plenty of vocations that don't have anything to do with employment. Our vocation, our calling, is to love God first and to love and serve our neighbor.

> For as in one body we have many members, and the members do not all have the same function, so we, though many, are one body in Christ, and individually members one of another. Having gifts that differ according to the grace given to us, let us use them: if prophecy, in proportion to our faith; if service, in our serving; the one who teaches, in his teaching; the one who exhorts, in his exhortation; the one who contributes, in generosity; the one who leads, with zeal; the one who does acts of mercy, with cheerfulness. (Romans 12:4–8)

God puts us in a variety of positions, so we have a variety of "neighbors" to love and serve. There are plenty of vocations in the family: parent, child, sibling, spouse, and more. There are vocations in our workplace. These may be the jobs we are paid for, but they could also be relationships in and around our job.

There are vocations in the Church, of course: pastors, teachers, organists, and other paid professionals, as well as volunteers like Sunday School teachers, choir members, ushers, funeral committee members, the people who fold the worship folders, and more.

There are vocations in civil life: voters and campaign workers, politicians and civil servants, lobbyists and grant writers. We can even have vocations in our hobbies. Just because we are having fun, that doesn't mean we can't be loving and serving our neighbor at the same time.

That is the beauty of vocation. We have the opportunity to love and serve others where we are. God puts us there for a reason.

In our Bible reading for this session, we have a glimpse of David's vocations. In 2 Samuel 5:3, we start off with his being anointed king. That's a pretty impressive vocation; it provides him with many neighbors to love and serve. But then we see where he can have a closer relationship. For instance, 2 Samuel 5:13 tells that he took more wives and concubines and he had sons and daughters—vocations of husband and father. Then, before we finish the chapter, we see David leading his men into battle in the vocation of general. But what stands out to me here is how he sought God's direction with every new battle. David's greatest vocation was being a child of God.

Read the following verses and identify David's vocation and whom he serves.

1 Samuel 16:21 armor bearer, Saul

1 Samuel 16:23 musician, Saul

1 Samuel 17:12 son, Jesse

1 Samuel 17:17–18 meal server, brothers/commander

1 Samuel 17:34–35 shepherd, Saul?

1 Samuel 17:50 soldier, God/Philistines?

1 Samuel 18:1 friend, Jonathan

1 Samuel 18:5 soldier, Saul, troops, officers

1 Samuel 25:40 husband, Abigail

2 Samuel 5:14 father, children

2 Samuel 6:14–15 King, praising God

2 Samuel 7:29 servant, God

2 Samuel 9 King, mephibosheth

1 Chronicles 11:1–3 King, God

1 Chronicles 22:1–5 Father, Solomon

Psalm 8 worshiper, God

1. In the Lord's Prayer, we pray, "Give us this day our daily bread" (Matthew 6:11). List as many vocations as you can that God utilizes to answer this petition. Start with the farmer who grows the grain.

   Farmer, Harvester, Truck Driver, Salesman, whoever cooks/prepares food

2. Let's talk about our vocations. What is the second-greatest commandment, according to Mark 12:31? How does this passage support the doctrine of vocation?

   love your neighbor as yourself, help others

3. As children of God, we know that we have been redeemed, saved by Jesus. He paid for every one of our sins on the cross. We can't do anything more to save ourselves. We can't improve on what God has already done for us. How does Galatians 5:14 speak to this? What are we to do in response?

   Be kind and loving to all. Do things to repair + maintain good relationships

4. Who is your neighbor? Read Luke 10:25–37.

   Everyone no matter race/religion, etc.

Journal Prompt

Today, think about your vocations. List each vocation you currently have, who benefits from it, how you love or can show love to each person within that vocation, and how it reflects your identity as a baptized and redeemed child of God.

MASKS OF GOD

Read Genesis 18:1–15.

When my children were young, I prayed, "God, help me to be a good mom." I thought this was a good prayer, a noble prayer. Then one day, after praying this, I thought, *That's not so noble; that's actually kind of vain.* I wasn't praying for my children as much as I was praying for myself. Not that praying for yourself is bad; it is good to ask God for things for ourselves as well as for others. But I had been thinking I was doing something for my children with that prayer. Then I realized that God is capable of bringing up my children without my help. There are plenty of children who grow up without a mom for whatever reason, and God uses other people to love them and provide for them. So I changed my prayer and asked that God provide for my children what they needed, like necessities, experiences, people, love, whatever they needed to encourage them to be faithful to Him and to grow up to be the people God wanted them to become. I am thankful that He chose to use me in their lives and that I was a part of their development. But I knew that God was raising them; He was simply using me to do it. Luther refers to this as a "mask" of God. God is doing His work but wearing me as a mask. When I live out my vocation as a mom, God is working through me and loving my children and bringing them up.

> God could easily give you grain and fruit without your plowing and planting. But He does not want to do so. Neither does He want your plowing and planting alone to give you grain and fruit; but you are to plow and plant and then ask His blessing and pray: "Now let God take over; now grant grain

and fruit, dear Lord! Our plowing and planting will not do it. It is Thy gift." . . . What else is all our work to God—whether in the fields, in the garden, in the city, in the house, in war, or in government . . . by which He wants to give His gifts . . . ? These are the masks of God, behind which He wants to remain concealed and do all things. . . . He could give children without using men and women. But He does not want to do this. Instead, He joins man and woman so that it appears to be the work of man and woman, and yet He does it under the cover of such masks. We have the saying: "God gives every good thing, but not just by waving a wand." God gives all good gifts; but you must lend a hand and take the bull by the horns; that is, you must work and thus give God good cause and a mask." (AE 14:114–15)

"Wow! You've done such a good job with those kids!" I can't help smiling when I hear that because I am very pleased with who my children have become. But I know, and sometimes admit aloud, that it is not my doing. God brought them to where they are today.

My grown children are involved in church work. Mark, the eldest, was ordained and is working as a campus pastor at a Lutheran high school. Nick, the second, is finishing his vicarage and will be returning to seminary for one more year before he is called to be a pastor. Angela is doing a yearlong internship as a director of Christian education at a church and then will be eligible to receive a call. People have asked what I did to inspire them to go into church work. The answer is that God did it. He used me as a mask. He also used other masks: an experience at a Christian camp encouraged Nick to pursue ministry; Mark's university professors inspired him to go to the seminary; and youth directors at our church gave Angela a heart for ministry.

In our lesson today, we see God using the mask of a stranger, the angel who told Abraham that Sarah would have a child. The interesting thing here is that we get to see the mask from the other side. In my story, God used me as a mask. In Abraham and Sarah's story, God wore a stranger's mask to minister to them. God's people today are blessed in this way also. We may not always recognize God behind the mask as Abraham did, but still God uses others. When Nick was a teenager at camp, God used the mask of a teenage girl. Nick didn't even talk to her. But it was when he saw her with tears streaming down her face in the moment when she understood that Jesus had won forgiveness and salvation for her that he first felt God's call to minister to His people.

Author Gene Veith explains the mask analogy well: "On the surface, we see an ordinary human face—our mother, the doctor, the teacher, the waitress, our pastor—but, beneath the appearances, God is ministering to us through them. God is hidden in human vocations" ("Masks of God," *The Lutheran Witness*, August 2001). So, in all of our vocations, we are used by God as His masks to show His love to others. Our vocation does not have to be big and exciting. God uses us in our mundane lives as well as our sophisticated careers to accomplish His goals.

1. Read Exodus 3:13–22. Who is going to bring the Israelites up out of the affliction of Egypt? Who was the mask?

2. Read Exodus 4:13–17. How do these verses illustrate the mask concept?

3. According to 1 Corinthians 12:4–7, what does Paul say about who is working through us?

4. According to 1 Corinthians 12:7, what is each of us given? Why? What does that mean to you?

5. Paul talks about our different gifts. No one has all of them; no one is called to do everything. What does 1 Corinthians 12:11 say? How does that apply to our discussion?

6. Read 1 Corinthians 10:31; Colossians 3:17; and Colossians 3:23–24. What do these verses say about our mundane or ordinary lives?

Journal Prompt

Yesterday you listed your vocations. Today, go deeper into one or two of them. How is God using you as a mask to love someone? Discuss what you are doing, who you are doing it for, your gifts and abilities that enable you to be a blessing, and how God is glorified through what you are doing. None of this has to be glamorous or highly spiritual; changing diapers is a vital task and very important to the recipient of your love.

DAY 3

SUCH A TIME AS THIS

Read the Book of Esther.

Note: Esther is only ten chapters long, but if you don't have time to read the whole book, read 2:5–18; 3:8–11; 4; 5:1–8; and 7, which describe her actions. However, you will have greater context and understanding of her story by reading the whole book.

When I was fifteen, I decided I was going to work in the Church. I had gone to a "Joy in Ministry" retreat and was on fire. I worked out all the details, including what colleges I would attend, and I started making it happen. Except that it never happened—not the way I planned it at fifteen. God did call me, as you've read; He just didn't call me to work in a church. (At least not yet!)

By the time I graduated from college, I was married and had no job prospects in the town where my husband worked and where we lived. When I was trying to decide what to do, someone asked, "Do you want to work in a church, or do you want to have a ministry?"

That was when I learned that God calls us to service everywhere. I started teaching in a public school in Las Vegas, Nevada, with children who had dramatically different life experiences than I had. My brightest student that first year had ambitions. His goal was to be a pimp. Sex and money—what more could a twelve-year-old boy want? Also that year, I taught a drug awareness unit, but this teacher's awareness increased more than any of the students'.

I had a room full of children who needed to be loved. Because I was in a public school, I couldn't outright tell them about God's love for them or tell them how He had died to atone for their sins. But I could *show* them love. Most knew I went to church. God brought the children to me, and I had the opportunity to serve the Lord by serving them. Instead of "going and serving the Lord," I was *staying* and serving the Lord.

God calls each of us—for a purpose. Whether we are in a sixth-grade classroom or a magnificent palace, we can reach out to someone with Christ's love. Queen Esther did not always live in a palace. She was an orphan, being raised by her cousin. God moved her into the palace and into the position of queen so she could be in a position to save her people. She may have grown accustomed to the beauty and luxury that surrounded her by the time she was asked to risk it all—to risk her own life. Going before the king uninvited was punishable by death if he did not feel kindly toward the uninvited visitor; that was risky enough. But the king in Esther's story was unstable. There was no predicting how he might feel at any moment.

But God is stable. God had taken years to place Esther for His purpose. This was the moment to which He called her. This was why she was in the palace and the queen of a vast empire. She was called to speak to the king on behalf of her people and save them from destruction.

The words Mordecai sent to her—"And who knows whether you have not come to the kingdom for such a time as this?" (Esther 4:14)—were recorded for all of God's people. Just as Esther was put in the palace for a purpose, God puts us where and when He does for His purpose. One of the primary lessons of this study is for each of us to ask ourselves:

Why has God brought me here?

What has He called me to do?

What are my vocations?

When I was fifteen, I had dreams of working in a church, but God called me to a secular classroom in one of the rougher areas of "Sin City" to love children.

1. Read Esther 2:5–8. What do we know about Esther at the time she received her "call"?

The Bible doesn't say how Esther felt about being taken into the king's harem or how she felt about the king himself. Sometimes we think of this as a Cinderella story—the young maiden becoming a queen. But consider that she didn't have a choice in the matter. She may have had other plans or other people in her life that her placement in the king's harem affected.

2. How do you think you would have felt or how might you have reacted if you had been Esther?

3. Read Esther 2:8–18. Regardless of how she felt about her position, what do we know about how she handled the initial change of career?

4. Read Esther 8:1–8. Most of what we have discussed has been Esther's call. But what was she called to do? Once God had her in place as the queen of Persia, what did she accomplish?

5. List the ways you think God has called you. This can be as big and dramatic as being queen of a vast empire so you can ask the king to save a whole race of people, or it can be as ordinary as taking care of a child. (I have a feeling that most of us have significantly more ordinary callings. But those are wonderful.)

6. Read Acts 1:8. Where does Jesus say that the disciples will be His witnesses? Read Acts 1:4. Where are the disciples when Jesus says this to them?

So often when we read Matthew 28:19, "Go therefore and make disciples of all nations, baptizing them in the name of the Father and of the Son and of the Holy Spirit," we focus on the "going" and the "all nations" and forget that Jesus also told the disciples that they were to be witnesses right there at home. Judea was their home. And Jerusalem was in Judea. We can witness at home and in the surrounding areas, or we can go to the ends of the world.

Journal Prompt

Look at your list of areas in which God may be calling you to be His witness. Choose one and write about how God may be calling you where you are, in your home, in your place of employment, or in other areas of influence for such a time as this. Write about how you can share His love and how He has died so that we can all live forever with Him.

DAY 4

STUMBLE

Read Mark 5:1–20.

Amy is one of those women who has it all together.

She is a sixth-grade teacher who also teaches teachers by regularly leading workshops and in-service programs for her colleagues. She also teaches at the local college on occasion. Amy and her husband have raised three children. She has taught Sunday School for adults, confirmation classes for children, and Bible studies for women. She has served on church boards and held various other positions in the congregation. She is held in high esteem by most in all areas of her life.

Then the Holy Spirit started nudging Amy to reveal some things that she would rather have kept hidden. Amy knew that God loved her and that He had forgiven her for all of her sins. That didn't mean she wanted to broadcast them. But it seemed to her that God wanted her to be vulnerable. When she learned that Hannah, a teenager in the congregation, was pregnant, Amy felt urged to talk to Hannah's mother and share her own story. After resisting for a while and then consulting with a few trusted friends, she asked to talk to Becky, the teenager's mother.

Amy confided that when she was a young unwed woman, she got pregnant. She panicked, moved across the country away from the father, and put the child up for adoption. But she didn't follow through with the adoption. After the child was born, she reunited with the father. They married and had more children together. The wonderful family that the congregation had watched grow and blossom had a very rocky start.

While the baby grew in Hannah's belly, Becky saw Amy and her family in church. For Becky, seeing them was a constant reminder from God that everything would be okay. She was reminded that God forgives and provides for His beloved children. That Amy was a wonderful woman of God with a lovely family was a tremendous comfort to the mother of this young girl. It gave her hope for her daughter. And the day Hannah's baby was baptized, Amy was at the Baptism, praying for the baby girl and her family.

> The Spirit intercedes for the saints according to the will of God. And we know that for those who love God all things work together for good, for those who are called according to His purpose. (Romans 8:27–28)

Years have passed. Hannah married the father of her baby and together they are raising their family and doing very well.

Sometimes it is not our victories that inspire others but our stumbles. Realizing that we are not alone, that others struggle with the same sins and situations we struggle with, can be encouraging. Sharing our struggles, failures, or weaknesses is not easy. In fact, it is very hard to be vulnerable. But if God calls you to share your confession with another, you can be confident that He will use it to bless that other person—and very likely you too.

How about you? Do you have a story to tell? Do the people who know you best, who know where you have been and the struggles you have endured, need to hear how God moves in your life?

You may not want to tell your story. It may be too painful or too embarrassing, something you would really like to put behind you. I imagine the man possessed by the legion of demons wasn't proud of that time in his life. After all, he ran around naked most of the time he was possessed. But to this day, his story continues to show us God's power over evil.

Consider that there is someone who would benefit from hearing about where you have been and how you have turned from a mistake. They especially need to hear how God has worked or is working in your life.

1. Read Mark 5:1–5 and Luke 8:27–29. Describe in detail the man who met Jesus.

2. What do you think this man's life had been like before this meeting?

3. Read Mark 5:6–15. What did Jesus do for the man?

4. In Mark 5:18, what was his response to Jesus?

5. Write what Jesus said to the man in Mark 5:19.

Here Jesus had a willing missionary—and He sent him home! Where would this man have the more powerful ministry? The people in the Decapolis had seen him for years. They knew what he was like and how hopeless his situation was. The people who already knew him would be much more moved by this miracle and the power of God than people in Judea who didn't know him. Jesus told this man to go home and tell people he knew what God had done for him. And that is exactly what he did.

6. What has the Lord done for you? How has He had mercy on you? Brainstorm and list things God has done for you.

Journal Prompt

Write your own psalm (or song) about what God has done for you using the list you brainstormed earlier and Psalm 66 as a guide.

DAY 5

SAYING YES TO GOD

Read Exodus 3:1–4:17.

Our two oldest children had gone to college. Tony, the little boy we had been raising, was back living with his mother, and we had one child left at home. That one, Angela, kept telling me how long it would be until she, too, would leave. I was feeling a loss of purpose. On the drive home from Bible study one evening, I talked to God about it.

"God, what do You want me to do?" I asked aloud. God didn't actually answer in words, but a thought came to me during the middle of that prayer.

"I could write," I said. "What should I write?" My mind went to manuscripts I had started and ideas I had come up with. There was a fun children's story I was hoping to work on; but no, that was not it. "I could write about home as a mission field."

I sighed. "I'm not sure what exactly to write about that. I don't know if there is enough material. How would I set it up? Lord, I know that You are the one with the message and that if I obey, You will take care of the details."

I concluded the prayer with the resolve to write a book that would be pleasing to God. I wasn't sure how to proceed. I wasn't sure what format to use. Would God really bless this, or was that just my imagination? About the time I would ask myself that, I would hear a sermon or read a Bible passage or hear something on the radio or experience an event that would illustrate why I was compelled to write this book.

I wrote more. Bit by bit, I drafted ideas for vignettes, an outline for the book, and a format. But I hesitated the whole way.

When God called Moses into leadership, Moses was not very excited about the prospect. In fact, I think Moses was terrified. He gave God a list of excuses why he couldn't do it and finally said, "Please send someone else" (Exodus 4:13).

God answered Moses' reluctance in many ways. Right away He told Moses, "I will be with you" (Exodus 3:12). Then God gave him words to say and signs to perform to convince the people that he was truly sent by God. God concluded by saying, "Now therefore go, and I will be with your mouth and teach you what you shall speak" (Exodus 4:12).

God called Moses to do something that Moses thought he was incapable of doing and did not want to do. But God was calling him to obedience. God had the plan; He knew what He was going to do and how He would accomplish it.

When Moses finally stepped in line to do what God asked, God used him to lead His people out of slavery and to the Promised Land. God performed many miracles through Moses and established a covenant with His people. All this because Moses was obedient.

How often do I want God to send someone else because I think I can't do what He is asking me to do? God can send someone else, but in His wisdom, He asked me. Don't I want to be obedient and see what God will accomplish through me? Instead of giving Moses' initial answer, "Please send someone else," I want to try and answer as Isaiah did: "Here I am! Send me" (Isaiah 6:8).

1. Look up the following Bible verses. Fill in the chart to show why the person God called didn't seem like a good choice—either to the person being called, or to the rest of us—and then note how this chosen one was able to glorify God.

   Judges 6:11–15; 7:20–23   Luke 1:26–34; 1:46–55
   Judges 14:1–4; 16:23–30   Luke 5:1–11; 9:18–20
   1 Samuel 16:1–13; 17:46–47   Acts 9:1–16; 19:11–12
   Isaiah 6:1–5, 8

Called Servant	Unlikely Choice	Glorified God by:
Gideon		
Samson		
David		
Isaiah		
Mary		
Simon Peter		
Saul/Paul		

2. Then there was Jonah. Read Jonah 1:1–3. What was his reaction to God's call?

3. Read Jonah 4:1–3. Why did Jonah run away from what God wanted him to do?

4. Read Jonah 3:1–5. What did Jonah accomplish by resisting God's call? What can we learn from this?

5. In Exodus 4:10, Moses told God that he wasn't a very good speaker and so he was not the right person for the job. What limitations do you have that you think keep you from doing something? Do you think God can use you in spite of those limitations or even because of them? Read Philippians 4:13.

Journal Prompt

Do you have something before you that seems too hard or beyond your capacity or expertise? Write about this in your journal. Ask God what He wants you to do. Ask Him to show you how He wants it done and to give you the wisdom to accomplish what He wants.

Called to Be a Child of God

So often when we think of missions or vocations or callings, we focus on what job or profession we think we should be doing. Our first calling is to be a child of God. God created us to be His children. Jesus died for our sins and redeemed us from destruction and eternal damnation. The Spirit lives in us and sanctifies us. As baptized children of God, we belong to Him. And because of who we are in Christ, others are blessed through us. In John 15, Jesus tells us that abiding in Him is how we bear much fruit. In other words, I am able to do great things because God does them through me. To me that is freeing. My value does not come from what I do or who I am; it is because I belong to Jesus that I have worth. This week we will look at how we can abide in Jesus and because of that, be used by God to be a blessing to our neighbors.

Memory Verse: "I am the vine; you are the branches. Whoever abides in Me and I in him, he it is that bears much fruit, for apart from Me you can do nothing." John 15:5

BOYS

Read 3 John 1–8.

I saw my friend Jean several pews ahead of me at church. She was at one end of a row, her husband sat close to the other end, and between them sat five high school boys. I smiled. What an awesome row. Mark and Jean have two sons; the three others were their friends.

These boys go to one of the roughest schools in town. They could have gone to a private school or transferred to a different public school, but their parents decided that South High School, with its honors program, was the best option for them. And it gave the boys an opportunity to be witnesses to other students in their school. Jean was involved in their school from the time they entered kindergarten until they graduated from high school. She volunteered in every capacity available to her. She also was able to talk to other parents about her love for Jesus.

Each week, there were several boys in church, and I don't believe it was always the same boys. Apparently, these boys weren't only in church. Mark and Jean opened their home and had their sons' friends as guests on a regular basis. It was because these boys were at that school and made friends there that they had the opportunity to let others see what Jesus meant to them.

The Bible story today is about a man named Gaius. He welcomed the missionaries and helped them however he could. There is another Gaius in the Bible that Paul mentions in Romans 16:23a: "Gaius, who is host to me and the whole church, greets you." Did you catch that? "Who is host to me and the *whole* church" (emphasis added). These may or may not have been the same man; in any case, Gaius knew how to open his heart and probably his home to help spread the Gospel.

Gaius made friends with these strangers, just like Mark and Jean's sons made friends. Through those friendships, God was able to do His work. God wore the mask of a teenage boy to bring His love to other teenage boys. God wore the mask of a friend to support missionaries in their work. God works in your friendships as well so that more people get to know the love of God.

Mark and Jean made a choice to send their children to public schools. The boys' presence in the school, as well as Jean's presence as a volunteer, gave them an opportunity to interact in the lives of people who might not have experienced Jesus any other way. The boys were simply going to school, learning, doing homework, making friends, and participating in activities. Jean was a band mom, a room mother, and a volunteer in other capacities. But as they were going about their lives, they were ambassadors for Christ. Just being who they were, they shared Jesus with others.

1. Fill in the blanks of this week's Bible verse, John 15:5:
    "I am the _____; you are the branches.
    Whoever _____ in Me and I in him, he it
    is that _____ much fruit, for _____
    from Me you can do _____."

2. According to John 15:5, what empowers us to do anything?

3. Look up John 15:5 in various translations. (A parallel Bible or Biblegateway.com is an easy way to access multiple translations.) What are some other words that are used for "abides"? What does it mean to "abide in God"?

4. Read 2 Corinthians 3:4–6. What does this passage say about where our abilities come from?

5. What does Galatians 6:9–10 tell us to do, and what will we gain from it?

6. Who does 1 John 3:1 say we are?

Journal Prompt

I have several questions for you to consider; respond to the ones that are most meaningful to you and skip the ones that don't apply. Do you abide in God? How so? Or if not, how could you abide in Him? As a result of abiding in Him, do you bear much fruit? What does your fruit look like? Do others see you as a child of God?

DAY 2

COME ALONG WITH ME

Read 1 Timothy 1:3–7; 3:14–15.

Tim sat in the back seat as his dad drove to visit a woman who couldn't get out much. Tim was excited to be going on a shut-in call. "How far is it to the lady's house?"

"Not that far." Dad glanced at him in the rearview mirror. "We're going to be there for a while. Don't ask when we can go; we'll go when it is time to go."

"Okay," Tim agreed.

"And you need to be polite. And respectful."

"Okay."

When they arrived, a lady Tim had never seen opened the door and let them in. Tim followed his dad in. The living room they went into reminded him of his grandma's house. Everything was clean and tidy. It even smelled like Grandma. He climbed up on the plaid couch and listened to his dad talk to the lady. His dad read the Bible and prayed with her. Then he gave her Communion.

She must be very special for my dad to come see her all by herself, Tim thought.

When Tim was older, he realized that she was very special—not because his dad, a busy pastor, visited her, but because she was a child of God and Jesus died for her.

As he was growing up, Tim went on quite a few shut-in calls with his dad, Kerry. He enjoyed these visits. Kerry was discipling his son from a very young age. Part of his job as pastor was to make calls to people who couldn't make it to church.

Early in his life, as Tim watched the impact his father had in his ministry, his own desire to be a pastor developed. Tim grew up, and he did become a pastor. He feels that geriatric ministry is a particular strength. Joining his father as he made calls might not have seemed like much at the time. Kerry might not have even considered what a difference it would make in his son's life. But spending time with his son while he performed one of his vocations impacted his son's life. Grown-up Tim said, "I would not be a pastor if not for my father."

Another Pastor Timothy had a similar experience. We read about him in our lesson today. There aren't many specifics about his upbringing, but the Bible tells us that his mother and grandmother were filled with faith and they passed that on to Timothy. They lived their lives of faith, and they taught Timothy the Scriptures. He was there to see it and grow in his faith.

When I started homeschooling, I quit going to Wednesday morning Bible study. I thought I didn't have time. But it didn't take long for me to realize that I very much needed Bible study. I devoted many hours of my day to educating my children, but I needed fellowship and time in the Word. So we started packing up the schoolbooks every Wednesday; the children sat at their own table and worked on schoolwork they could do independently, and I sat at another table with the other women in the study. The children weren't as productive during those two hours, but the blessings they received from being there far outweighed what they had to make up in math or language arts. They were loved on, and they heard the praises sung to God and the devotions that were read for the whole room. They were given opportunities to stand in front of the ladies and recite their memory work. All I did was bring them along on my own faith walk.

> Go therefore and make disciples of all nations, baptizing
> them in the name of the Father and of the Son and of the
> Holy Spirit. (Matthew 28:19)

As we live as children of God, others come along with us. They see God in our lives.

For our study today, we are going to look at John Mark. His story is not in a neat little package of verses. We have to jump around the New Testament to piece together what went on in his life. But it is exciting.

Read Acts 15:36–41.

1. What were Paul and Barnabas planning? What problem came up? How was it resolved? What was actually a silver lining about this resolution?

2. Let's back up and see what inspired this disagreement. Read Acts 13:5, 13. (Remember, we are reading about John Mark. These passages use the name John, but it is the same man.) What happens in these verses?

3. What do we learn about John Mark's relationship with Barnabas in Colossians 4:10?

Paul and Barnabas are called by the Holy Spirit to go on a missionary journey. They bring Barnabas's young nephew, John Mark, along. He helps out for a while, but then for reasons undisclosed, he abandons the mission and returns home. When it is time for a second missionary journey, Barnabas wants to take his nephew again, but Paul wants nothing to do with that. So Barnabas heads out with his nephew and goes back to Cyprus, where John Mark had been before, and Paul chooses a different companion and goes to Syria and Cilicia.

4. Look at Colossians 4:10 again and 2 Timothy 4:11. What can you glean from these two passages about Paul's feelings for Mark after the young man had had a chance to mature?

5. What did Mark write that shows that he did indeed mature and was working to spread the Gospel?

Barnabas took the time and energy to take his nephew under his wing. He brought him along on missionary journeys and, like young Tim, he wasn't much help initially. But by being exposed to the work and the life, he grew into quite a leader.

Journal Prompt

Is someone watching you live your life? Does that person see you studying your Bible, worshiping, receiving the Sacrament, and praying? Does he or she see you making choices based on God's Word rather than what the world presents? Does he or she see you reaching out to others and loving God's people? Does this person know that your vocation as a child of God is very important to you? Write a prayer in your journal. Ask God to be with this person who may be watching how you live your life. Ask God to fill him or her with His Spirit and be present in that person's life. Ask God to fill you with His Spirit so people can see Jesus in you and so you "bear much fruit," or are productive in your efforts to share Christ through your vocations. Pray specifically about the interactions you have with this disciple.

DAY 3

DIVINE APPOINTMENT

Read Acts 8:4–8, 26–36.

Paige helped plan the youth mission trip to Japan, but as she did, she had this nagging thought that she shouldn't go. As one of the youth leaders, though, accompanying the group was part of her job. So she tried to dismiss the feeling of doubt and kept moving forward.

The feeling wouldn't go away.

She prayed and searched Scripture. And Paige came upon Acts 16:6–10. Paul and Timothy kept being redirected by the Holy Spirit. Wait. *What?* Paul and Timothy had been prevented from ministering? Sometimes God wants us to *not* do something? Was it possible that God did not want her to go on this mission trip?

About four months before the trip, she got up her nerve and told her ministry partner her thoughts. They worked it out so a teacher from the church's school would go instead. This teacher was an ideal choice; she had even lived in Asia when she was younger.

Then Paige's parents contacted her with an invitation. They wanted to visit with Paige and her husband, Patrick, sometime that summer. As they worked through schedules, it became apparent that the only time they could all meet was the same time as the Japan trip. Paige felt awkward about the timing. She worried that it looked like she skipped out on the mission trip so she could go on vacation.

As the youth group was in the air, flying to Japan, Paige and her husband were driving to Denver to visit with her parents. They stopped for lunch, and Paige got a phone call from her sister-in-law, Christina.

Christina's grandma was nearing the end of her life. This rocked Christina, and she wanted to talk to Paige about spiritual things. Paige had often shared her faith with Christina. This time, Christina came to her. She needed answers to questions like "How do you know if you are saved? if you are going to heaven?" Paige told her that "if you confess with your mouth that Jesus is Lord and believe in your heart that God raised Him from the dead, you will be saved" (Romans 10:9). The two women talked a long time, concluding with a prayer in which Christina confessed her faith in Jesus as her Savior.

Paige was so glad that she was not on an airplane, away from her cell phone, when her dear friend and sister-in-law needed her.

Paige and Patrick were still in Denver when they got word that Patrick's grandmother had passed away. His grandparents lived in Denver, so they went to be with Patrick's grandfather and were able to help with arrangements, attend the funeral, and even sing at the service.

Paige had thought she was going to go to Japan and minister to students there, both those who went on the youth trip and those who live in Japan. But she believes that God had other plans for her. He wanted her in the United States so she could minister to her sister-in-law, her husband, her husband's grandfather, and the rest of the family. Sometimes the things God calls us to do don't look very "spiritual" at first. But God knows what people need, and He knew that Christina and Patrick and Grandpa and many other people would need Paige's love and presence. He worked it out so she could be there for them.

> Many are the plans in the mind of a man, but it is the
> purpose of the Lord that will stand. (Proverbs 19:21)

In Acts 8:4–8, we see Philip busy doing God's work in Samaria. Then, in verse 26, an angel tells him to go down the road to a desert place. If it had been me, I might have been tempted to say, "I'm already busy doing the Lord's work." I would have told the angel about the important things I was doing and suggested that someone else go. I would have at least wanted to know what the purpose was. But Philip was told to go, and he went. It wasn't until he got there that he was shown what to do. He was already working for God in Samaria. But God had a different plan for him.

How open am I to God changing my plans? I was in the habit of rising in the morning and telling God, "Okay, this is what I need to accomplish today. Help me get it done." Then a friend told me she would get up and say, "Okay, God, show me what we are going to do today."

My first response was that I couldn't do that; my schedule was so booked that I didn't have time to be flexible. But then I realized that I *could* change my plans and that things would go better if I opened up my plans to God's direction instead of asking Him to bless *my* plans.

Read Acts 11:19–21.

1. What happened to the followers of Christ after Stephen was martyred?

2. What did God do with the scattered people?

3. What was the eternal result of the people being scattered?

4. Read Romans 1:8–15. What does Paul say he wants to do? Why didn't he do it?

5. Paul eventually did make it to Rome. Read Acts 25:11–12. Under what circumstances was his travel arranged?

6. What did God say to Paul in Acts 23:11?

From the time Paul was arrested in Jerusalem until he left for Rome, he had the opportunity to testify, telling his story and the story of Jesus at least six times. That sounds like a divine appointment.

Journal Prompt

Think of a time when your carefully laid plans were interrupted, changed, or delayed. Could this have been a divine appointment? Think back on the details of the situation. Why weren't you able to complete your plans the way you had made them? What happened because of the change of plans? Did God want to show you something, or did He want you to minister to someone else?

DAY 4

JUST ME

Read Mark 10:13–16.

It was dark when my mom dropped me off in the church parking lot. I got out of the car and headed into the church office. I had gotten word that our pastor was leading the youth Bible study in his office this week, so I bounced on in. The door was ajar, but I didn't hear much noise coming from the office. I waited a bit, listening for the voices of my friends or movement inside. The pastor came out and saw me. "Come on in, Cathy."

I went into his empty office. "No one else is here yet?" I asked.

"I don't know if anyone else is coming," he said as he pulled up a chair.

I was a little confused. If no one else was coming, surely he would cancel the Bible study. But he indicated that I should have a seat.

I sat on the edge of the chair opposite him and asked, "So are we just going to wait until next week, when more people are here?"

"Well, you weren't here last week, were you?"

I shook my head.

"We can go over last week's lesson and catch you up, and then next week we will go on when everyone else is here."

I was surprised. Here was the senior pastor of a large church leading a Bible study one-on-one with a seventeen-year-old girl. I knew he had more significant things to do, but the hour this important man spent with me made a lasting impression. His actions said that I was valuable enough to help me try to understand part of the Book of Revelation. I felt inconsequential because of my age but even more so because there was only one of me. It would have made more sense if he had waited to share his knowledge with a group of high school students. My pastor, however, didn't think that way.

The disciples thought like I did. They didn't want Jesus' time wasted by blessing children one by one. But Jesus knew that each and every child there was special and deserved His time. More than that, God the Son knows that each and every one of us is valuable—so much so that He willingly paid for our redemption with His own blood. That is some kind of special.

We sometimes think that it takes numbers to make an impact in ministry. And there are times when our ministry is to tens or hundreds or thousands. But sometimes our ministry is one-on-one with a valuable, precious child of God. We should not discount the one. If my pastor had said that since I was the only one there, we were canceling Bible study, I would have been fine with that. I would have called my mom to pick me up and not thought twice about it. But the fact that he valued me and showed me that God values me has caused me to remember that time often over the past thirty years. I remember only a bit of the study we did, but I have never forgotten how my pastor showed me that I counted for something.

Read Psalm 8.

1. The first three verses are full of praise for God, detailing how magnificent He is. What question does the psalmist ask in verse 4?

2. Even though God has set His glory in the heavens, are *you* important? How do you know? Verses 5–8 will help you answer this question.

3. Read John 5:1–9. How many invalids were there at Bethesda? Could Jesus have healed all of them at once? How many does the Bible record Jesus healing at that time?

Read Mark 5:21–34.

4. Who comes to Jesus in verse 22 to ask for help? State his name and position. Was he an important person?

5. Who interrupts Jesus as He is on His way to save the little girl? Did she seem to believe that she was worthy of Jesus' time?

6. What did Jesus do that conveyed that He wasn't too busy for her but that she was indeed important and that He cared for her?

Journal Prompt

Who is one person you can help and to whom you can demonstrate that he or she is valuable to you and to God as well? Once you have decided who that one person is, how can you show Christ's love to that person?

DAY 5

ACCIDENTAL MASK

Read Exodus 2:1–10.

"Do you know who Moses is?" Pastor D. asked. "He was the one who parted the seas," Tony answered quickly.

Jack wasn't going to be outdone. "He was a baby and his mom and sister wanted to save him, so they put him in the water."

"And the Pharaoh's daughter saved him out of the water and said she would keep him," Tony finished the thought.

I sat with the two boys in the pastor's office. Jack, our foster son, wanted to be baptized. Pastor D. had asked to speak with him. What started as a regular pre-Baptism meeting turned into a "who knows the Bible best" competition between ten-year-old Jack and eight-year-old Tony.

"Wow, you boys really know your Bible stories," Pastor D. commented. He seemed genuinely pleased. The most impressive part was that Jack had lived with us for only about three months; before that, he'd had no religious instruction of any kind. I confess to feeling a little proud as I sat there while these boys recounted Bible story after Bible story. The truth was that I had very little to do with their extensive knowledge. It wasn't like I had told them these stories. What I had done was require them to read something for at least thirty minutes each day before they could play video games. One of their favorite choices was an illustrated Bible story book. It was easy reading and had lots of cool pictures. Both boys had read the whole book.

The next week, Jack was baptized. The following week, he received Communion for the first time with his class. Only a few weeks after that, he left our home. I was sad and confused. When we took Jack in, we had planned for him to live with us until he was at least eighteen. I wondered why God had put him with us if it was only for a few months. What had we done wrong? Then I thought about what God had accomplished while Jack was with us. He put Jack in a place where there were ample materials to give him exposure to His Word. He saw to it that Jack was able to go to both Sunday School and Vacation Bible School. He orchestrated the timing of the First Communion class and put the desire into Jack's heart to be baptized. God put us in Jack's life for a season, and then He would put on a different mask to continue His work in Jack's life. I had thought we had years to teach Jack about God and all the other things we thought were important; God knew we had just a few months and made the most of the time Jack was with us. I was oblivious to how short our time with Jack was—but God wasn't. He used our family to make a difference in Jack's life.

In our Bible story for today, God used a princess mask to accomplish His purposes. Moses should have been killed along with all the other baby boys of his time. Instead, his mother tried to save his life. Pharaoh's daughter found him, took him home, and raised him in the palace. God knew the plans He had for Moses. He had already chosen Moses to lead the children of Israel out of Egypt, through the desert, and to the Promised Land. To do that, Moses would need to be educated, trained to be a leader, and given the opportunity to acquire military skills. So God put on the princess mask, sent Moses to the palace, and saw to it that he got an unparalleled education as a prince of Egypt. That princess had no clue what God was planning to do with her adopted son. But God used her just the same.

You don't have to be skilled, intelligent, purposeful, or even willing for God to use you. Pretty much all my husband and I did was agree to take in a foster child. God did the rest. I see it so clearly now. We thought we were doing something for this little boy. What we did was so minuscule in comparison with what God did. And although we aren't in his life anymore, God is, wearing a different mask through other people.

1. Read Acts 7:20–22. This is Stephen's summary of the story we read earlier in Exodus. Look especially at verse 22. What value was there in Moses being raised by Pharaoh's daughter rather than his own mom?

2. According to Exodus 2:6, why did Pharaoh's daughter take an interest in the baby and take him to be her own? Was it so she could raise up a future leader of the Hebrew people who could lead them out of Egypt? Exodus 1:22 gives added motivation to consider.

3. Let's look at another woman in this story: Moses' mother. Look at Exodus 2:1–9. What actions did she take? What benefits did she gain from her actions?

4. Read Genesis 15:13–14. What did God tell Abram would happen centuries before Moses was born?

This is one of my favorite stories in the Bible. We get to see how things that appear to happen totally "by chance" and "accident" actually take place according to God's very carefully designed plan. More than four hundred years before our story began, God revealed the plan to Abram, which means this revelation occurred before any of his sons were born. There was no nation yet. There were no children yet. Centuries later, when the time was right, Moses was born into a world of great oppression for the Hebrews. He was supposed to be killed for the "crime" of being male. But his mother couldn't bring herself to obey the law and kill him, so she took the risk of hiding him. We can only imagine how difficult it was for Jochebed as she made that basket and prepared it for her baby. Some commentaries suggest that she was deliberate about trying to get him into the princess's hands. I think Jochebed was living from day to day, doing the best she could. God, on the other hand, was purposeful in all He was doing. He led the princess to the river that day. He gave her a soft heart toward the crying baby in the basket. Then, in a really exciting part of the story, the princess hired Jochebed to care for her own baby. Our hero goes to live with his Hebrew mother for those early formative years. At that time, children were nursed longer than they are today. Moses could have lived with his birth mother for as long as five years. Once his mother had a chance to influence his character, he went to the palace, where he received a prince's education and learned how to lead people, equipping him to lead the Hebrew people for forty years. No, this is not a story of "chance."

5. Let's look at what happened decades later, when the grown-up Moses returned to Egypt and demanded that Pharaoh let God's people go. Read Exodus 9:13–21. In verses 15–16, what does God say He could have done? Why didn't God do this?

No, you don't have to be skilled, intelligent, purposeful, or even willing for God to use you. He will accomplish what He wants to accomplish and do it through you. Pharaoh was in no way willing to be used by God to show the Creator's power and have "His name proclaimed in all the earth." In contrast, my husband and I *were* willing to be used by God, but we were clueless as to how quickly things would be accomplished. But God put it all there for Jack in a timely manner.

Journal Prompt

Look back at your life and your relationships. In retrospect, can you see how God used you to make a difference in someone else's life even though you were unaware how much of a difference it was making? Can you see how God used you as a mask to love someone in a way you had not set out to do? Reflect on that time. Give praise to God for what He did through you. If you can't think of such a time, write a prayer. Tell God that you are willing for Him to use you. And give praise to God for what He can accomplish through you, even if you aren't skilled, intelligent, purposeful, or even willing.

Called to Do Easy Things

I love the story of Gideon. Israel needed a strong victory against the Midianites, and God chose a weak man to do the job. To emphasize His point, God took an army of thirty-two thousand men and thinned it out until there were only three hundred. God was clear about what He was doing; He wanted it known that He was the one who won this battle. He didn't want human pride getting in the way of the credit going where it should. Then Gideon led these three hundred men to the enemy camp, not with swords but with trumpets and jar-covered torches. This unassertive leader of an unassuming army went against the mighty Midianites. Gideon and his men followed God's simple directions and, by His power, accomplished a huge victory. It would have been easier on their minds to keep all thirty-two thousand warriors and march down there with swords and spears. But when we see God working through the small and seemingly insignificant things He asks us to do, we see ourselves as part of His incredible victories. This is exciting to me because I realize that God can use even me to do marvelous things.

Memory Verse: "And let us not grow weary of doing good, for in due season we will reap, if we do not give up. So then, as we have opportunity, let us do good to everyone, and especially to those who are of the household of faith." Galatians 6:9–10

DAY 1

USED BY GOD

Read Judges 6–7.

Angela and Christian were friends. They spent a lot of time together throughout school. They carpooled to and from school, had most of their classes together, and were both in school plays. They saw a lot of each other—until Christian went to a different high school. Then, even though they lived only a mile and a half apart, they rarely saw each other. Angela had no idea what was going on in Christian's life. But after several months, she felt a strong sense that she should write him a letter. It took a couple of months, but eventually she wrote and mailed the letter. Christian responded; they got together, talked, and hung out.

Several months later, Christian shared with Angela what had been going on in his life. After he switched schools, he started hanging out with a different group of friends; he experimented with alcohol and marijuana, and he let his grades drop. Worst of all, he tried to push God out of his life. It was while he was away at a Christian camp that he challenged God: "If You really love me, bring Angela back into my life." He returned home from camp and from his challenge to God to find Angela's letter. God did love him.

God knew what was going on in Christian's life. He was there with him, providing for him, protecting him, and working toward the time when Christian's heart and mind would be reopened to Him. Months in advance, long before Christian had given God an ultimatum, God planted it in Angela's heart to write to him. She found other things to keep her busy but finally got it done at just the right time—in God's time.

Angela had the privilege of making a difference because she was obedient to the Holy Spirit's prompting. She was able to touch another life in a mighty way—in a way that she could not have accomplished by her own power, had she tried. When we open ourselves up to be used by God, we sometimes can see when God does mighty things.

> His strength within my weakness Will make me bold to say
> How His redeeming power Transforms my stubborn clay;
> His touch of fire ignites me, With courage I am sent,
> My tongue-tied silence broken, With grace made eloquent.
> (*LSB* 835:3)

We see in today's Bible reading that God did mighty things through Gideon because he was obedient. In both of these stories, it is evident that God was the one doing something. He moved normal, everyday people to be obedient, and through their faithful obedience, He accomplished big things, life-changing things that these people could never have accomplished on their own, even if they had tried as hard as they could. All they did was be obedient to God's direction, and God made things happen.

1. What did the Lord say to Gideon in Judges 6:14?

2. What qualified Gideon to lead an army? Gideon's résumé is in Judges 6:15.

3. Read Judges 6:16. Why was Gideon a good choice for this job?

An interesting thing about the judges—and all of the stories in the Bible, for that matter—is that the people God used to accomplish His will were flawed. We know from the story of Adam and Eve that all of humanity is sinful and condemned. God's Law calls attention to our flaws so that we understand both His divinity and, more to the point, our need for rescue. Rather than seeing Bible characters as role models, we see how God used them despite their deficiencies to accomplish His plan to bring about our salvation.

4. In Judges 13:2–5, the Lord calls another judge. What were the qualifications, indicated in 16:6, of this judge whom God used to deliver Israel? And where did these qualifications come from?

Judges 13–16 tells Samson's story, which is a mixture of his incredible strength and crippling weakness for women. We shouldn't see our weaknesses as something that will limit God. He uses us however we are; sometimes it is because of our weaknesses that we are the best choice for the job.

5. Read 2 Corinthians 12:9–10. What was Paul boasting about and why?

6. Where did Paul's strength come from?

Journal Prompt

Last week's lessons asked us to do something that we thought was too hard. This week's lessons are about God asking us to do something easy. Has God asked you to do something easy? Does it seem insignificant or awkward? Are you dragging your feet? Do you think it has been too long ago since He asked you to do it so He probably doesn't want you to do it anymore? Write about what God has asked you to do and what your first steps in obedience will be.

DAY 2

SPAGHETTI DINNER

Read John 6:1–13.

"We just got home from the hospital," my friend Tennie said over the phone. "Rebekah is doing better, just tired. We all are."

"I will bring you dinner," I volunteered.

"That isn't necessary."

Tennie's daughter had severe asthma. Hospital stays were common and exhausting for their whole family. When they were at the hospital, they were not home for the regular things like laundry and making dinner. I thought that not having to make dinner might make things a little easier for them.

"Really, it is not that big a deal. I am already making a big pot of spaghetti sauce. I will set some aside for your family, and all will be good." It really *wasn't* a big deal. I always make big batches of spaghetti sauce and then freeze it so I can pull it out at a later date. I doubled up on the side dishes and voila! Dinner for two families.

Later Tennie told me that it was an encouragement to her that I brought dinner that night. She could have made dinner, but not having to was so wonderful. I have been there. There have been times when someone has brought us a meal. Having that burden lifted from my shoulders was always a relief. The amount of work it took me to make dinner for my friend and deliver it does not even come close to the relief it was to her. And since that time, I have noticed on numerous occasions that Jesus takes the small things I do for others and magnifies them into tremendous blessings.

When we pray "give us this day our daily bread," we are asking for that day's food, of course. But in this simple request, we are also asking for everything necessary to sustain us bodily: shelter and clothing and even good government. Those things are made possible because God chooses to make them possible, and they are magnified according to His will.

In the Bible reading for today, a boy possessed a small thing that Jesus magnified. His five loaves of bread and two fish were the means by which Jesus provided for the people. Alone, even all we have doesn't amount to much. But in the hands of God, the smallest bit of obedience can accomplish more than we can ever imagine. Jesus can take my meager little offering and feed thousands with it. Remembering that makes me excited about doing for others, even when it seems so insignificant, because I trust in God's creative power.

1. What was Andrew's analysis of their resources for feeding so many people in John 6:9? What was his opinion of the boy's lunch?

2. What did Jesus ask Philip in verse 5? And why was He asking Philip this?

3. Jesus put the task before the disciples and gave them a chance to contemplate how to solve the problem. Since John tells us that Jesus already knew what He was going to do, why do you think He asked Philip where to get bread?

4. This is not the first instance of God taking a little and using it to feed many. Read 2 Kings 4:42–44. How much bread was provided to feed how many men?

5. Look back at verse 38. What was going on at that time?

6. What did the man from Baal-shalishah say when Elisha told him to give the bread to the men? What percentage of the men did Elisha feed? Did they have enough to eat? How do you know?

Sometimes God shows us how hopeless a situation is first, and then He wows us with His awesomeness.

Journal Prompt

Think about a time when someone did something small for you that meant a lot to you. Maybe it was praying with you, sending a well-timed card, or offering a word of encouragement. Maybe it was serving a cup of coffee or a meal. Reflect on how Jesus magnified this person's simple act so it was a blessing for you. Think back over the last week or month and describe how another person has reflected Jesus' love and mercy to you. Then read Martin Luther's explanation of the Fourth Petition of the Lord's Prayer in the Small Catechism. Include both that individual's small act and the Lord's blessings to you this week in your journal entry.

JESUS LOVES ME

Read John 8:3–11.

"Jesus loves me, this I know," Susie sang. She knew Jesus loved her; everyone said so. Besides, what's not to love? She held on to this truth as she grew—until she got a divorce. Then Susie wondered if Jesus really did love her. She was consumed with guilt and went to her Bible for comfort. She found passages like 1 Corinthians 7 that spoke against divorce and said a wife can be the way a husband comes to know Jesus. Guilt was piled upon guilt. She carried this burden with her everywhere.

Then one day, Susie was buying gas for her car. As she got her change, she looked at one of the bills; "Jesus loves you" was scrawled on it. She stared at that bill and let the meaning sink in. Jesus loved *her*. Jesus died for *her*. Yes, she had made some mistakes. But it wasn't because she was a cute little kid singing "Jesus Loves Me" that He died. It was because she was a sinner that He died. And because of His death, she was redeemed.

Sometimes we need the Law to smack us in the face to really appreciate the Gospel. Without the Law, we can't appreciate the magnitude of God's love for us. If we are perfect, why wouldn't He love us? But if we have disappointed Him or others, His love is a very impressive thing. Susan knew her divorce was not pleasing to God, but she learned that God loved her anyway.

When our sin is overwhelming, as with the woman caught in adultery in our lesson today, we need to hear that we are forgiven. This woman had no doubt that she had sinned. If she had any doubt, the

Pharisees were present to make sure she knew she was worthy of death. Once Jesus had dealt with the Pharisees, He turned to the woman to teach her that He wasn't there to condemn her—that she was worthy of His love and forgiveness.

One of the most well-known verses in the Bible is John 3:16: "For God so loved the world, that He gave His only Son, that whoever believes in Him should not perish but have eternal life." Read those words again. These words are for you and me, sinners though we are. They are also for the people around us whose sins may be even more noticeable to us. There is a reason the verse is so popular. When we are feeling the weight of our guilt and sin, it is a mighty powerful thing to keep reading. "For God did not send His Son into the world to condemn the world, but in order that the world might be saved through Him. Whoever believes in Him is not condemned" (John 3:17–18a). When we are overwhelmed with our own guilt as Susan was, we need to hear that Jesus still loves us. When we recognize our failures and repent, we enjoy the full benefit of Jesus' forgiveness. This is why, early in the Divine Service, we make a public confession; speaking these words prepares our hearts and minds to receive the Words of Absolution spoken by the pastor "as from God Himself, not doubting, but firmly believing that by it our sins are forgiven before God in heaven" (*LSB*, p. 326; SC, Confession, question 266).

1. Let's get down to the nitty-gritty right away. According to Romans 3:23, have you sinned? How do you know?

2. Now continue reading Romans 3:24 and then turn to
   Romans 6:23. What do we learn here?

I know that Jesus loves me. I know that He saved me from my sins.
I have heard this Gospel message since I was a child. Yet I still find myself
tripping over my sins. If I think about it, I know that God has forgiven
me. But sometimes when I don't think about it, I let my failures make me
feel unworthy and unloved. Yes, I am unworthy, but I am most definitely
loved beyond my wildest comprehension of love. God has forgiven me
and claimed me as His own. If I can forget this when I have heard all of
my life about the love God has for me, then what about the person who
hasn't heard that message? Susie knew that Jesus loved her—until she
started doubting. Even though she had been taught from an early age
about Jesus' love for her, her sins pointed out her unworthiness. She
needed to be reminded that Jesus loved her despite any and all of her
sins. Many people are like the woman in our story. They don't know that
Jesus loves them, but they are keenly aware of their own unworthiness
to stand before a just God. They need to hear that Jesus loves them, and
they need to hear it more than once.

3. What does Jesus tell us to do in Mark 16:15?

4. Read Ephesians 2:4–5. What is the Gospel of Jesus Christ?

5. Read 1 John 4:7–12 and fill in the blanks below.

Beloved, let us _____ one another,
for _____ is from God, and whoever
_____ has been born of God and knows
God. Anyone who does not _____ does not
know God, because God is _____. In this the
_____ of God was made manifest among us,
that God sent His only Son into the world, so that we might
live through Him. In this is _____, not that we
have _____ God but that He _____
us and sent His Son to be the propitiation for our sins.
Beloved, if God _____ us, we also ought to
_____ one another. No one has ever seen God; if
we _____ one another, God abides in us and His
_____ is perfected in us.

Journal Prompt

Make a list of people you know who need to be reminded that Jesus loves them despite their sin. Take to heart the apostle Paul's words: "Be kind to one another, tenderhearted, forgiving one another, as God in Christ forgave you" (Ephesians 4:32). Pray over your list and then proceed to let those people know that Jesus does love them very much. Send one of these people a card and write a word of encouragement that includes John 3:16 and as many other verses as are appropriate.

DAY 4

A WORD FITLY SPOKEN

Read John 4:1–45.

"What are three things that made your week great?" our friend Scott asked my daughter, Angela. While she was answering his question, I thought about how I had heard him ask this of other people on numerous occasions. What a fantastic conversation opener. Scott is a vibrant, go-get-'em kind of guy. Just about every time we see him, he tries to engage Tony in one way or another. Ten-year-old Tony often shuts down around strangers, but Scott isn't a stranger for long. He has repeatedly asked Tony about great things going on in his life or his baseball team or his girlfriend (which of course Tony denies having).

One Sunday we were sitting in our usual spot in church and there was a new family sitting in the row in front of us. Before the seats had a chance to warm up, Scott was there. "Hi! My name is Scott." He shook hands with both of the parents and then turned his attention to the junior high-age boy. "What school do you go to? Do you like your teacher? Oh, you have several teachers? Well, which one is your favorite?"

From my vantage point, I couldn't hear what the boy said, but I could hear Scott. I was mesmerized as I watched him work. He had a knack for asking questions that gave the other person a chance to express himself. And most important, he listened to the answers.

Jesus' conversation with the Samaritan woman started with a command: "Give Me a drink." To us today, that request for a little water seems simple enough. But to the woman at the well, His straightforward appeal was the jumping-off point for a full-blown theological discussion.

Jesus' thirst was an opportunity to talk with this woman. What did Jesus say when His disciples returned with food and encouraged Him to eat? He told them that His food was "to do the will of Him who sent Me and to accomplish His work." So, no, asking for water was not about His own need; it was about hers. He told her He was the long-awaited Messiah, which was news she rushed to share with the rest of the village. As a result, many people came to know Him as the Savior of the world.

> Many Samaritans from that town believed in Him because
> of the woman's testimony. . . . And many more believed
> because of His word. (John 4:39, 41)

Just one little conversation starter and a whole village was introduced to Jesus the Christ. Because He is God, Jesus has a way of multiplying blessings. But we can follow His lead and start conversations with strangers. Having a few questions ready can be a great tool for getting people talking and can even lead to deeper discussions. Who knows? We might be able to introduce someone to Jesus.

1. Read Jeremiah 29:12. What does God say He will do when we pray to Him?

2. In John 4, what evidence is there that Jesus listened to the Samaritan woman?

3. Read Mark 9:17–27. What does Jesus ask the father? Do you think Jesus didn't know the answer to this question? If not, then why would Jesus ask the question?

4. Jesus gave the father a chance to tell his story. And Jesus listened. What words did the father say in Mark 9:24 that captured the wrestling he had been doing between his hopelessness and his belief that Jesus could make a difference? Can you think of a time when you wrestled like this?

5. Read Proverbs 25:11. What is like "apples of gold in a setting of silver"?

Journal Prompt

Write out Isaiah 50:4a, then brainstorm some questions you can have ready to ask people that you meet, that you want to meet, or that you have already met and want to start a conversation with. It is fine to start your list with Scott's question: "What are three things that made your week great?" But then go from there and put your own personality into the questions.

DAY 5

SOCIAL MEDIA

Read Colossians 4:2–18.

My phone beeped, indicating that I had received a text. It was from my oldest son. "Please pray for my friend Caleb and his wife, Kristen. They were in a bad accident." That was all I needed to see. I went to God in prayer and asked Him to be with Mark's friends. I didn't have to know all the details or what specifically they needed. I knew only that they needed prayer. My prayers were going to the One who knows all things: what happened, how they were hurt, where they were, and what needed to be done for them. I prayed to the Great Physician, who could heal them and provide doctors and other health care professionals to attend to them.

After I finished praying, I checked social media with the intent of posting a prayer request. Another of Caleb's friends had posted a prayer request. She had a little more information—their car had rolled several times, and Caleb's brother had seen the whole thing from his own car. I posted another prayer request on my own page and asked my friends to pray for this couple that most of them did not know at all.

Mark texted me again. He shared the info that I already had from Facebook and also told me that the couple had been on their way to St. Louis, where Caleb was going to seminary to study to be a pastor. I took several deep breaths and dialed the church phone number. The last time I called with a prayer request for friends involved in an accident, I cried so hard I couldn't talk. This time, I kept my composure until I provided all the information, holding steady until almost the end. My voice cracked when I said the couple had been heading to the seminary.

I got on social media again and there were several "likes" and comments about people praying for these friends of Mark's. I also saw a link to Caleb's brother's post on Caleb's page, updating his friends. I went to his page for his brother's report about the accident and about them being airlifted to a bigger hospital.

Sometimes social media is criticized as being a waste of time, frivolous, and even unhealthy. I have seen plenty of posts and comments that are ugly or hateful. But these instruments can serve a purpose. After Caleb was better and out of the hospital, he posted a message on his own page:

> Just wanted to let everyone know that my wife and I are ok. I just now went through all 200 something of my notifications and I am humbled and in awe of all the love and support and prayer that we were wrapped in during our experience. You all have shown us that the church of God and community of believers can get together and pray for people they don't even know and God can and will move mountains.

I imagine that there were thousands of people praying for them. What a powerful thing to have that many people in prayer for you. And what a wonderful use of social media. I will often see prayer requests on my feed. How long does it take me to bow my head and lift a person or situation in prayer? It certainly takes less time than watching a video about some silly thing a cat did or clicking on a meme to see a joke or personal philosophy.

> What a friend we have in Jesus, All our sins and griefs to bear!
> What a privilege to carry Ev'rything to God in prayer!
> Oh, what peace we often forfeit;
> Oh, what needless pain we bear—
> All because we do not carry
> Ev'rything to God in prayer! (*LSB* 770:1)

In the Bible reading for today, Paul asks for prayers in general and for specific prayers for himself and his team. Then he sends greetings and asks that his letters be shared with the Laodiceans. A major part of Paul's ministry was conducted via letters to churches he visited. Can you imagine what Paul would have been able to do with social media? Yet Paul's words in the Bible have been seen and read by more people than could ever be reached through social media. Like all inventions and means of communication, social media is a tool we can use for God's glory. In addition to being a prayer chain, it is used by youth ministers to communicate information about events and opportunities. People use it to post Bible verses and devotions. We can use it to learn about missionaries and their work throughout the world. Social media is an easy way to share how God is working in our own lives. What is seen by many as a mere distraction can be used for a higher purpose.

1. Let's turn to the Bible passage that talks about how we are to use social media. Read Colossians 3:17. What does this verse tell us about how we should use this form of communication?

2. It is always good to read things in context. So let's back up and start at Colossians 3:12 and read through verse 17. What if everyone approached social media this way? Make a note of the things in this passage that are helpful when posting messages and sharing links.

3. Look up the following verses: Colossians 4:2–4;
   1 Thessalonians 5:25; 2 Thessalonians 3:1–2; Philemon 22;
   Hebrews 13:18–19. What is Paul saying in all of these verses?

4. How can we follow Paul's example? Think of some specific
   ways you can use social media in your own life.

5. Read Colossians 4:7–17. What does Paul say in this
   passage? Can you do something similar on social media?
   Describe an example in your own life.

Journal Prompt

Use some form of social media to give glory to God. Stretch yourself.
If you are new to this medium, you might just copy a Bible verse to post
or ask for prayer. If you use social media all the time, try to use it in a way
that you never have before. Maybe you can make your own meme. Or try
a new app. But do something different as you lift up the name of Jesus.

Write a prayer thanking God for the various ways His Word is shared
today and asking His blessing on your own use of technology to share
your faith and witness to His mercy, provision, and promise of salvation.

Called to Stay Home

The Proverbs 31 woman is far more precious than jewels. She is worthy of praise and is held in high esteem. But the interesting thing about her is that she is based at home. It is not that she doesn't work outside the home, but the actions listed in Proverbs 31 have to do with how she cares for those in and around her home. She might even be called a housewife, which gives me a lot of encouragement. I have often felt intimidated by this woman and yet she is "just a housewife" like me. It makes me realize that the things I do at home matter; they are worthy of praise. In the concluding litany of all this amazing woman does, the author says, "She looks well to the ways of her household and does not eat the bread of idleness" (Proverbs 31:27). This week we will explore the mission field of our home. We will investigate how we can make an eternal difference in the lives of those closest to us, those we love most.

Memory Verse: "Charm is deceitful, and beauty is vain, but a woman who fears the Lord is to be praised." Proverbs 31:30

FAR MORE PRECIOUS THAN JEWELS

Read Genesis 2:4–24.

When my husband, Steve, and I were first married, I tried to please him by baking for him. One day when he came home, I surprised him with a plate of warm chocolate chip cookies. Our little apartment was filled with the aroma of my efforts.

Steve barely noticed. He set his bags down and went to the desk to look for something in a drawer. I followed him, holding the plate.

"I made cookies."

He glanced at me and nodded.

"Do you want one?"

"Not right now. I'm looking for some papers I need for school."

"Don't you like baked goods?"

"Yeah, they're fine. I'm just busy right now."

I took the plate back to the kitchen and took a cookie with me to the couch. Disappointed that my surprise didn't go over better, I took a bite of the cookie. *Well, even if he doesn't like it, I do.*

This wasn't the first time I had baked for him and he hadn't seemed excited. I started thinking about what I was doing wrong, and the thought occurred to me: *as crazy as it sounds, maybe the way to my husband's heart is not through his stomach.* Instead of doing things for him that would please *me*, I had to think about what would please *him*, what *he* needed. At that moment, getting up and helping him find his papers was a good idea. I had another epiphany that Saturday afternoon: maybe the wifely duties that my husband needed were not typically performed in the kitchen.

That happened more than thirty years ago. I still remember it because it changed how I went about ministering to my husband. I started looking for what he needed instead of what I wanted to give him. They are two very different things. There are times that I do minister to him in the kitchen. Other times ministry can take the form of a picked-up living room. Other rooms that see active ministry are the laundry room and the bedroom.

But mostly, I think God wants me to be there for Steve as a refuge, someone who loves him, encourages him, and believes in him. In Ephesians 5:33, after several verses of Paul telling men to love their wives, he concludes, "However, let each one of you love his wife as himself, and let the wife see that she respects her husband."

Respect. One of the main things that my husband needs is my respect. I do have a lot of respect for Steve; frankly, there is a lot to respect. But I am not always good at showing it to him.

Proverbs 19:14 tells us: "House and wealth are inherited from fathers, but a prudent wife is from the LORD." I am a gift to my husband, a gift from the Lord. And as Proverbs 31:10 tells us, "An excellent wife . . . is far more precious than jewels." How cool is that?

Now, as I lift my husband in prayer, I ask God how best to minister to this man He has put in my life.

1. As God created the world, what is the recurring theme in Genesis 1:4, 10, 12, 18, 21, 25, and 31? What is the problem in Genesis 2:18?

2. Read Genesis 2:18–24. What was the solution to the
   problem presented in verse 18? What was tried before a
   satisfactory solution was found?

God knew what He was doing from the beginning. This scenario
played out the way it did for Adam's benefit. First, man was shown that
he was in need. Then God showed him that none of the creatures already
created would fill that need. Finally, God provided a solution that was
beyond what Adam could imagine.

The first vocation women were called to was being a wife. So those
of us who are wives can look at it as a calling from God.

3. Look up the following Bible verses and summarize what
   God says about wives.

   Proverbs 12:4

   Proverbs 18:22

   Proverbs 19:14

   Proverbs 31:10

4. Look up these verses and write what we should be careful to not become.

   Proverbs 19:13

Proverbs 21:9

Proverbs 27:15–16

5. We started reading in Proverbs 31 about an excellent wife. Let's read the whole passage, verses 10–31. As you read, list the specific things this excellent Hebrew wife does. Then, next to each item, jot down how this does or could translate in your life.

6. Now read these verses and write what else the Bible says we can do in ministry to our husbands.

    1 Corinthians 7:1–5

    Ephesians 5:33

    Colossians 3:18

    Colossians 3:23–24

    1 Timothy 3:11

    Titus 2:3–5

7. The most perfect picture of marriage is of the divine Bride-groom, Christ, and His Bride, the Church, given to us in Ephesians 5:25–27. Jesus gave Himself for us, sanctified us, and washed away our sin in the water and word of Baptism. This relationship is the model for earthly marriage. Carefully read these next two passages and summarize how a wife can make an eternal difference in her husband's life.

   1 Corinthians 7:12–16

   1 Peter 3:1–6

Journal Prompt

Write a prayer for your husband or future husband. Ask God to show you ways you can minister to him and receive ministry from him.

If you are not married, write a prayer asking God to bless you in your vocation as single woman and guide your footsteps as you seek to walk closer with Him through worship, Bible study, prayer, and service.

A HUNDREDFOLD

Read Matthew 13:1–9, 18–23.

"But it displeased Jonah exceedingly, and he was angry. And he prayed to the LORD and said, 'O LORD, is not this what I said when I was yet in my country? That is why I made haste to flee to Tarshish; for I knew that You are a gracious God and merciful, slow to anger and abounding in steadfast love, and relenting from disaster.'" I read aloud from my Bible. My children were sprawled around the living room while I read. A twelve-year-old boy, a ten-year-old boy, and a seven-year-old girl were trying to not fall asleep. Or maybe they were trying to sleep without me noticing. We tried to study religion in the morning when we were all together. From there, they had different assignments or activities. Sometimes, though, they weren't fully awake for our study of Scriptures.

We were reading the Bible chronologically at the same time as we were studying ancient history. It was fascinating to put the two together. For example, after reading about what the Assyrians were like, we felt more compassion for Jonah and understood why he didn't want to go to them and tell them to repent. His reluctance wasn't a matter of not wanting to do what God wanted or of being afraid they would laugh at him. He truly didn't want any good to come to them. And for good reason; they were despicable.

I homeschooled my children for most of their elementary and high school years. Sometimes things went great. Other times, I threw myself on the bed and sobbed for fear I was ruining them.

Looking back, I don't think I ruined them. They have all graduated from high school, and each was honored as valedictorian of the charter school we were part of. Each was admitted into an honors program and received scholarships to their university of choice. My oldest son graduated from university with honors, has completed his first year of seminary, and plans to become a pastor. My second son has just gotten married. He has also graduated with honors and will also go to seminary to become a pastor. My daughter received a scholarship that covered almost all of her tuition and has completed her first year of college. She plans to be a director of Christian education.

I don't take a lot of credit for their success. I think my role, in part, was to not get in the way of God's path for their lives. Yet I have felt guilty that spending so much time with my own children meant I wasn't doing God's work. I had planned to go into full-time ministry, work in a church, and touch countless lives. As it turned out, I spent the bulk of my time with just a few people.

But like the farmer in our Bible story today, I scattered seeds. And some of that seed fell on good soil. I may never go into full-time church work. But I have raised three children that are headed in that direction. So I see how the seeds I scattered can produce a hundred times what was sown.

> "Hear then the parable of the sower: When anyone hears
> the word of the kingdom and does not understand it, the
> evil one comes and snatches away what has been sown
> in his heart. This is what was sown along the path. As
> for what was sown on rocky ground, this is the one who
> hears the word and immediately receives it with joy, yet he
> has no root in himself, but endures for a while, and when
> tribulation or persecution arises on account of the word,
> immediately he falls away. As for what was sown among

thorns, this is the one who hears the word, but the cares of the world and the deceitfulness of riches choke the word, and it proves unfruitful. As for what was sown on good soil, this is the one who hears the word and understands it. He indeed bears fruit and yields, in one case a hundredfold, in another sixty, and in another thirty." (Matthew 13:18–23)

My son who is at seminary told me to look up a sermon in Luther's Works: "But this at least all married people should know. They can do no better work and do nothing more valuable either for God, for Christendom, for all the world, for themselves, and for their children than to bring up their children well" ("A Sermon on the Estate of Marriage," AE 44:12).

According to Martin Luther, there was value to my ministry. There were many, many days when I did not feel important, when I was sure I was a waste. But now I see how the seeds I planted have grown so much and continue to flourish. After my son directed me to Luther's words that nothing is more valuable than to bring up my children well, I understood. Being a mom is important ministry with far-reaching impact.

1. An inspiring person in the Bible appears in Exodus 2 (not the princess, but the other woman). Her "job" lasted only a few years (probably five at the most), but the effect that she had continues to this day. What did she do that made such an impact on the world?

2. Despite the short amount of time Jochebed had with her son, how was she able to make an impact on his life? See Exodus 2:11; what phrase is used twice in this verse? What became of her son when he was grown? See Exodus 3:9–10.

3. Jochebed's ministry to one has gone out to billions. Identify and briefly describe two or three other people in the Bible whose ministry to one reached many more. Why are you drawn to these people?

4. Another woman in the Bible had her son only until he was weaned. See 1 Samuel 1. Who was she? Who was her son? What became of him? (Read 1 Samuel 3:19–20.)

5. See 1 Samuel 2:12–26. After being weaned, Samuel was left in the care of Eli. Was Eli a model parent? What were his sons like? (You can read what became of Eli's sons in 1 Samuel 2:27–36 and 4:11.)

6. What we do with our children in the few years we have them does matter. Write Proverbs 22:6 below, and then explain what it means in your life, with your children. If you don't have children, what might it mean in the lives of children to whom you are important?

7. Read Deuteronomy 6:4–9. What are we to teach children and how are we to teach it? How can you apply this in your life?

Journal Prompt

Write a prayer about your children. Start by turning Psalm 127:3–5 into a prayer and thanking God for blessing you as He has. Then ask for guidance in bringing up your children in the way they should go. Ask Him to help you show your children how to love Him with all their heart and soul and might. Then pray for each child specifically as you see needs in his or her life. If you don't have children, ask God how He wants to use you in your family or in a specific child's life and how these individuals could benefit from your love.

DAY 3

HOSPITALITY

Read Luke 10:38–42.

"My girlfriend and her parents will be stopping by tomorrow," my son announced. "They are coming from church so they should be here around noon."

"Oh, okay," I said calmly. "Why don't you invite them for lunch?" It seemed like a logical action since they would be driving for a while and would arrive at mealtime. This would give us an opportunity to get to know this girl and her family a little better.

Later, the thought struck me, *WHAT will I serve them?* I couldn't possibly serve them what I would give to my own family. Panic set in. My mind raced as I tried to figure out what I had or could get and prepare after church to have ready when they arrived.

Finally, I settled on the menu: we would have a brunch. I picked up the necessary ingredients and hurried to put everything together.

Shortly after they arrived, we sat down to an egg dish, sausage, muffins, potatoes, sliced strawberries, and juice. I hoped everyone else enjoyed these things, but I didn't taste a thing. It went in my mouth and down my throat, but I couldn't taste it. I had been too busy trying to impress, or at least not have to hang my head in shame, to enjoy the fruit of my labor.

I can tell you that my son did not care at all what we ate. In fact, he probably didn't taste it either. All he was interested in was seeing his girlfriend and spending time with her.

I do not have the gift of hospitality. But I try to show hospitality. Romans 12:13 directs us: "Seek to show hospitality." What I always seem to forget is that hospitality is not about the food or the decorations or how clean the house is. It is about fellowship.

But like many, I am a lot like Martha in that I get lost in the business of hospitality and forget why I am being hospitable. Jesus said that Mary chose what is better. Mary got it. When Jesus came to visit, all she cared about was spending time at Jesus' feet, taking in everything He said.

The most important display of hospitality is the meal we receive at the Lord's Table, where Jesus gathers us, gives us Himself, and sustains us in faith. Each time we join with other believers at this meal, we do so not for the food but for the joy of receiving our Lord's very presence. I don't care what kind of wine my church uses. I am there to be in fellowship with Jesus. To kneel in His presence.

> Martin Luther tells us, "Herein the Sacrament you are to receive from the lips of Christ forgiveness of sin. It contains and brings with it God's grace and the Spirit with all His gifts, protection, shelter, and power against death and the devil and all misfortune." (LC 5:70, p. 439).

Sometimes I feel like it was a little disrespectful to Martha, seeing as she was working so hard to prepare a meal for Jesus. But Martha could have prepared that meal *and* spent time with Jesus if she didn't have to make sure that every little detail was perfect.

Martha may not have even tasted the delicious food she prepared, but she was definitely caught up in the preparations and lost sight of the true purpose of the visit, which was to spend time with Jesus.

1. Was Martha totally off base? What do the following verses say about hospitality? Note what Peter says our attitude should be like.
    Romans 12:13

    1 Peter 4:9

2. Copy Hebrews 13:2. Then read Genesis 18:1–8 and 19:1–3. Give examples of the Hebrews verse.

3. Gaius was also known for hospitality. Paul mentions him in Romans 16:23, and John writes a letter to him encouraging him to continue this hospitality. Read 3 John 1–8, focusing on verses 5–8. What does John tell Gaius that shows his hospitality is a ministry opportunity? To whom is Gaius ministering?

4. Look at your answers to questions 1–3. To whom are we supposed to show hospitality?

5. Jesus is coming for a visit. He will be at your front door exactly one hour from now, and He will be staying through the next meal. How will you spend the next hour? What will you serve Him, and what will you do while He is at your home? Now compare that to your answers to the same questions if the guest were a new person at your church.

Journal Prompt

What does hospitality look like today? What does God want us to do, and how does He want us to go about it? Abraham and Lot invited strangers in. That doesn't seem all that safe today. It wasn't safe in Lot's world for the strangers to stay outside. Gaius hosted a church in his home and took in church workers. Martha and others in the New Testament invited friends and loved ones to their home. Jesus invites us to receive Him in the Sacrament of the Altar. Write a prayer asking God how He is calling you to be hospitable and how to go about showing hospitality.

HONOR YOUR PARENTS

Read Mark 7:1–13.

It was early, and I wanted to make sure my dad got inside the building before I went on my way. His procedure would take a couple of hours, so I planned to have breakfast with my son. The two-hour drive had put me close to my son's university, so he was going to meet me halfway.

I pulled up in front of the doctor's office. I had lost count of how many times we had been here, and I knew that there were many more visits to come. My dad had surgery to remove his stomach and would have another surgery to reconnect the digestive tract so he could eat again. Today he would have a simple procedure to open a passageway that was a temporary necessity between the two major surgeries. I watched my dad walk to the door of the doctor's office and reflected: six months ago, he was strong, independent, and self-sufficient. Since then, cancer, treatments, and surgery had stripped a lot of that from him.

It was so early that the door was still locked. My dad came back to the car and got in, and then he pulled some money from his wallet and offered it to me.

"What's this for?" I asked.

"Parking and breakfast."

"Dad, you don't have to pay for my breakfast."

"Well, it's cheaper than if I had taken a bus or something."

I laughed. "A bus." Like I would have let my dad take a two-hour bus ride to his doctor's appointment in the heart of Los Angeles. I don't even know if he could have found a bus to take. It seemed ludicrous, but

I knew it was his way of holding on to a little bit of independence. He had to let me drive him, but he was going to provide all he could: the car, gas, parking, even breakfast.

Just then someone opened the door of the office building. My dad dropped the money on the seat and headed back inside.

There comes a time when people who took care of us need to be taken care of. And it isn't usually convenient for us, but it is less convenient for them. It is difficult to let go of independence and let others help you.

During Jesus' time, the Pharisees were not honoring their parents, as is commanded in the Ten Commandments. Of course, being Pharisees, they made a show of following the law, but they devised a loophole that allowed them to keep their possessions and not be obligated to use them to help their families. The tradition of Corban allowed someone to set aside any of their possessions by dedicating them to the temple. The actual transfer would happen when they died, so they could continue to use their possessions for themselves and protect them from being used to help others.

In the first century, there were no tax-funded care programs like we have today, of course. The elderly depended on their children to take care of them. If they didn't have children or didn't have children who would help them, they were reduced to begging or depending on the generosity of others for assistance.

> But if anyone does not provide for his relatives, and
> especially for members of his household, he has denied the
> faith and is worse than an unbeliever. (1 Timothy 5:8)

In our day, honoring our parents looks a little different, but it is still a command from God, and we need to figure out what that looks like in our families. In this case, as strange as it sounds, taking my dad's money was a way of honoring him. I drove him to the doctor, which honors him. And allowing him to still feel independent, needed, and in control was accomplished with twenty dollars. But honoring my parents has not always been easy. In fact, I have struggled with it most of my adult life.

My mom worked to destroy my marriage and enlisted the help of my dad. As this was happening, I searched Scripture for guidance; honoring my parents was a command, but Jesus also said, "What therefore God has joined together, let not man separate" (Matthew 19:6). These two things seemed to be in direct opposition with each other.

As I prayed and read my Bible, I concluded that obey and honor are different things. I didn't have to do what my mom was wanting, but I could still honor her. Sometimes that was merely not speaking ill of her. When she was slandering my husband and me, I wanted to fight back. I wanted to tell everyone the truth. Even as people were thinking ugly things about us, I was honoring her by holding my tongue. That little thing was very hard, and I wasn't always good at it. But now I thank Jesus that He has forgiven me for the times I failed. He has paid the price for my sin. He died for me.

1. We are commanded to honor our mother and father, however that looks for us. Read Exodus 20:12; Leviticus 19:3; and Ephesians 6:2–3. What message is God getting across here?

2. According to Deuteronomy 27:16, how strongly do you think God feels about this command?

3. Read 1 Timothy 5:3–4. What does Paul say about the children and grandchildren of widows?

4. Continue reading 1 Timothy 5:3–8. Paul has strong words about taking care of your family. What does he say about those who don't?

5. James 1:27 doesn't refer directly to parents, but what can we learn in connection with today's lesson from this verse?

6. Read John 19:23–27. How does Jesus honor His mother in verses 25–27?

Journal Prompt

Write about your parents and their specific needs. Then list ways you can help with those needs and thereby honor your parents. My dad was not in need financially. His needs were more in the way of logistics and respect. Respect is definitely a way many parents can be honored. That may include just holding your tongue. Your parents may be young and healthy and not seem to need anything. Would they feel needed and be honored if you asked their advice, for example? Don't forget the cliché to "call your mom."

If your parents are no longer living, are there other older family members or neighbors who would benefit from something you can do for or with them? Does your congregation have a ministry to seniors that you can participate in or support somehow?

CROWN OF THE AGED

Read Genesis 48:1–22.

Carolyn bowed her head to pray. The topic heaviest on her heart was her grandchildren. She loved being a grandma and she loved her grandchildren. Nine-year-old Ryan and eleven-year-old Zachary were the delight of her life. She prayed for them every day. "God, please be with Ryan and Zachary. Please convince their father that they should be baptized. I talked to the pastor today and he told me that their father needs to take an active role. Please put it on Michael's heart to pursue this. I feel like this is urgent." Her heart hurt.

Carolyn loved her grandchildren so much and their faith life was important to her, but she knew it wasn't important to Michael. Michael had been hurt by the church when he was a child; he had felt rejected by the leaders of the congregation. But to Carolyn, this wasn't about a church building or the people in it. It was about her grandchildren's eternal souls.

She helped Michael however she could, and she was always there for the kids. She took them back-to-school shopping, and they had a lunch date every other weekend—the weekend their father had them. Every summer, they went to Vacation Bible School, and she had occasionally gotten them to go to Sunday School. They knew they couldn't spend the night on Saturday unless they went to church with her the next morning because Grandma was at church every Sunday.

Carolyn was there for whatever needs her grandchildren had. Most of all, she prayed for them daily. This was her most important job as a grandma. She enjoyed their lunch dates, even if it was just fast food. She enjoyed taking them to the park or having them come over and play with

Zoe, her puppy. But she knew that what they needed most was to know Jesus and understand that He loves them and that He died so they could live forever with Him. In his Small Catechism, Martin Luther says that babies are to be baptized because they "are included in the words 'all nations'," and he follows that by giving us the words of Matthew 28:19: "Go and make disciples of all nations, baptizing them in the name of the Father and of the Son and of the Holy Spirit" (SC, Question 303, p. 288). It was of great concern to Carolyn that her grandchildren remained unbaptized.

In our lesson today, we see the blessings of a grandfather. Joseph brought his sons to his father, Jacob. Jacob laid his hands on his grandsons' heads. This wasn't according to tradition or the way Joseph would have had him do it, so he tried to redirect his father. But Jacob was adamant. Jacob, being a younger son himself, gave the younger son the greater blessing. It was a grandpa's pleasure to bless his grandsons, and he blessed them in the way he wanted. I can imagine the twinkle in old Jacob's eye and the frustration on Joseph's face. What fun to be a grandparent to bless and be a blessing to those special people we love.

> What do you think? If a man has a hundred sheep, and one
> of them has gone astray, does he not leave the ninety-nine
> on the mountains and go in search of the one that went
> astray? And if he finds it, truly, I say to you, he rejoices over
> it more than over the ninety-nine that never went astray.
> So it is not the will of My Father who is in heaven that one
> of these little ones should perish. (Matthew 18:12–14)

The value of Grandma's prayers can be seen from a different angle. Bethany, in her first year away from home, was overwhelmed. College classes, choir, drama practices, roommate issues, and social life worked together to make her life feel like it was coming apart. Sleep? There was no time for sleep. When Bethany felt most overwhelmed, she remembered that her grandma was praying for her every day. That fact—and she knew it *was* a fact—gave her enough strength to face whatever had to be faced at that moment. Bethany was quite capable of praying on her own, and she did so quite often. But knowing that her grandma was always praying for her was much more encouraging.

Whether or not they fully comprehend it, Ryan and Zachary have that same blessing. Their grandma is praying for them every day. That in itself is mighty and powerful. But they also know that their grandma has a strong faith in God. They know how important her faith is to her. And there may come a time when knowing their grandma is praying for them is the encouragement they need to face what seems impossible. They have a most special gift, a praying grandma.

1. According to Proverbs 17:6, what are grandchildren?

2. What is another way we receive a crown? See James 1:12. How might this relate to being a grandparent?

3. According to Psalm 103:17, how can a grandma's faith be a blessing to her grandchildren?

4. What do the following verses say about our prayers?
   James 5:16

Proverbs 15:29

Psalm 145:18–19

5. Read Psalm 102. What does the psalmist say in the midst of his prayer, in verse 18? Even if you don't have grandchildren, how can you minister to future generations?

Journal Prompt

Write a prayer for your grandchildren or your future grandchildren or the parents of your future grandchildren or the descendants of someone you know and love. If you have a godchild, send that person a card or a note that reminds him or her of the blessings of Baptism. Pray that they know and love the Lord and that He blesses them unto eternity.

Called to Shine Like Lights

Crooked, twisted, warped, perverse, perverted, hard, and corrupt. These are all words used in different translations of Philippians 2:15. The ESV says it this way: "Do all things without grumbling or disputing, that you may be blameless and innocent, children of God without blemish in the midst of a crooked and twisted generation, among whom you shine as lights in the world" (Philippians 2:14–15). Those are some harsh words Paul uses to describe our world. He is right, of course. In that kind of setting, children of God would definitely shine forth like lights. God has called us to this broken world. He has called us to live in it and make a difference. He has called us to shine as His children and glorify Him in our lives.

Memory Verse: "You are the light of the world. A city set on a hill cannot be hidden. Nor do people light a lamp and put it under a basket, but on a stand, and it gives light to all in the house. In the same way, let your light shine before others, so that they may see your good works and give glory to your Father who is in heaven." Matthew 5:14–16

DAY 1

SHEEP IN THE MIDST
OF WOLVES

Read Jeremiah 1:4–10; 26:1–15.

Missy was a freshman in high school. She had a Sunday School faith, but she was quiet and meek. She wasn't the kind of person who would evangelize other students; she didn't feel she knew enough for that type of thing. But she knew with all of her heart that God loved her and that Jesus had died on the cross to atone for her sins.

Early in her freshman year, Mr. Schaffer, her journalism teacher, asked Missy, "Did you read that article on Islamic terrorism?"

"Yes, I did," Missy said.

"What did you think? Was it bad that this woman wanted to blow herself and other people up?" he looked at her, waiting for an answer.

Is he serious? she thought. Aloud, she said, "Yeah, it's bad. We aren't supposed to take anybody's life. It says that in the Bible."

"Well, this woman believes in god," the teacher countered.

Missy didn't hesitate. "Well, her god is not our God. Allah is not God."

Mr. Schaffer smiled. "That's what I want you to write an article about."

Missy did just that. She wrote an article for the school newspaper differentiating God from Allah.

The day after the newspaper came out, Missy arrived at school to find her article on God and Allah posted all over the school. Some students had made copies of it and had written across the top, "If this isn't racism, what is it?" This little article, written by a freshman, might have gone unnoticed by most of the student body. Instead, these protesters brought it to the attention of just about everyone on campus.

A few students found Missy online and harassed her. These reactions to her story only strengthened her. She *knew* she wasn't racist, so those comments served only to reinforce her position. She also didn't want to get caught off guard, so she just studied more and spent more time in her Bible.

Later in the year, Missy was talking with another student in her journalism class. Whitney was as well-known an agnostic as Missy was a Christian. Whitney pointed to Missy's textbook. "What's the deal with that?"

Missy looked at where she had drawn all over the book cover. "Those are Bible verses I like. And I drew some crosses too."

Whitney shrugged. "Yeah, I don't believe in that."

Missy considered how this mattered in her everyday life. "Well, my little sister died. When I pray, it gives me peace."

Whitney nodded, and Missy figured that was the end of that.

A few years later, the two students were seniors. They didn't have any classes together, so they didn't interact much. But one day, when Missy saw Whitney in the hall, she said, "Hey, how are you doing?"

Whitney said, "Missy, I want to tell you something. Remember a long time ago when you said you prayed after your family member died? Well, my uncle died recently, and I remembered what you said. I prayed, and you were right. It gave me peace."

Missy was happy. While she was sad that Whitney's uncle died, she was thrilled that Whitney had remembered her words and thought to pray to God and that her prayers brought her some comfort.

In today's Bible reading, we saw Jeremiah being called by God. Jeremiah's first response was that he was too young to speak God's

Word. Missy—and many other young people—feel the same way. Missy said, "As a teenager and a student, it can feel kinda weird 'cause you're not a pastor and you're not a teacher, and so it almost feels like that job has been put on you."

God's response to Jeremiah was "Do not say, 'I am only a youth.'" God used Jeremiah to take His message to the people. Missy could learn from those words as well. God used her as a mask to reach other teenagers. She was able to communicate with Whitney in ways that no pastor or teacher would be able to do. And her article, although criticized harshly, was read by many of her classmates. Jeremiah's message wasn't received very enthusiastically, but he shared the message God gave him to share.

What can we gain from these examples? We can be assured in any circumstance that if God gives us something to say, we can say it with confidence and He will be there with us. We may not feel strong or significant, but God will use us to share His message with people who wouldn't listen to someone high and mighty.

> If you cannot speak like angels, If you cannot preach like Paul,
> You can tell the love of Jesus, You can say He died for all.
> If you cannot rouse the wicked With the judgment's dread alarms,
> You can lead the little children To the Savior's waiting arms. (*LSB* 826:2)

Read Matthew 10:16–20. I see Missy as a sheep that went among the wolves at a public high school. She was as wise as a serpent. (She had studied her Bible and was inspired to study even more when she came up against opposition.) She was also as innocent as a dove. (She was not a racist, not hate filled. She was a sweet young believer, telling the truth.)

1. What does verse 20 tell us about the mask of God?

Read Psalm 107:1–3. Write verse 1 on a card or slip of paper that you can keep with you and look at frequently. This passage is a reminder of where we can start with our evangelizing, with a heart that rejoices in God and knows that He loves us.

2. In verse 2, who are "the redeemed of the LORD"? See Hebrews 9:14–15.

3. What does Psalm 107:2 say that we, the redeemed of the Lord, are to do? And what does that mean?

4. Read Psalm 103:1–5. List the ways God has redeemed us that are mentioned in these verses.

Journal Prompt

What has God redeemed you from? Here is the answer we can all give: He died on the cross and saved us from our sins. He has taken our punishment so we can live eternally in paradise with Him. But I'm looking for a more personal answer: How has He saved *you*? What could you tell an unbeliever that God has done for *you*? You, who are redeemed of the Lord: What do *you* have to say? Write in your journal how God has redeemed you.

DAY 2

GOD'S TOOLS

Read 2 Samuel 23:8–39.

We had barely finished saying grace when my husband looked at me and said, "Do I have 'Tell me your life story' tattooed on my forehead?" The children looked at his forehead, checking for a tattoo. I smiled because I knew where this was going. "All I did was ask one of my students if she was okay and she burst into tears."

"No," I said, "there is no tattoo. But did you pray that prayer again? The one in which you ask God to use you?"

"Yeah, I did." He looked down at his plate and scooped some mashed potatoes onto his fork.

"What did you think was going to happen? You ask God to use you, He's going to use you. No tattoo necessary." Steve acts like it is a problem, having students come to him, confide in him, and seek his guidance. But the truth is that he knows that listening is a special trait of his. And he is willing to have God use him in the lives of his students.

In his thirty-plus years of teaching, Steve has come in contact with thousands of young people. That is mind-boggling to me. Most of those years have been in public schools where teachers are not allowed to bring up matters of faith. Yet the students still know. You don't have to have a tattoo for the students to see Christ in you.

Most of the students never let him know what impact he has had on them. But a few do. One particular student wrote Steve a letter, years after she was his student. She confessed that because of his talks with her and because he saw her as valuable, she decided not to commit suicide.

She also told him that she had become a Christian (he knew she had not been brought up in a Christian home).

Today we read about David's mighty men. These men were warriors, all loyal to David. They had a job to do, and they were used by God to accomplish amazing things. Josheb-basshebeth killed eight hundred men at one time with a spear. That rivals most action movies I've seen. Three of the warriors broke through enemy lines for the sole purpose of getting a drink of water for David. But the two we will focus on are Eleazar and Shammah. These men stood alone against an untold number of Philistines and didn't relent until they had struck down their enemy. The verses that tell us the most are verses 10, "And the LORD brought about a great victory that day," and 12, "and the LORD worked a great victory." These verses emphasize that although these men did amazing things, it was God who accomplished the victory. God was wearing the mask of a warrior.

Wherever we work, whatever our job, we can be God's tools. We can be available to be used by God to bring about a great victory. Even if our job is in a place that is hostile to Christianity, we can figuratively break through the enemy lines and retrieve a glass of water for our King. Pray that God uses you in your place of work, then watch as He brings people to you and works a great victory through you.

1. Steve prayed that God would use him. According to Romans 6:13, what are we to present our members to God as?

2. Depending on your occupation, your work environment can be one of the hardest places to share the love of God. What does Romans 12:1–2 say about this?

3. Read 1 Corinthians 6:19–20. Why are we supposed to glorify God with our bodies?

4. Read 1 Peter 1:18–19. What was the price paid for you?

5. To bring this idea home, write out Hebrews 9:12.

6. What are we enabled to do through the blood of Christ?

Journal Prompt

Here more than anywhere, the secular and the Christian definitions of vocation come together. We are talking about your vocation within your work setting. In this session, we've seen a teacher and soldiers serving their neighbor as they carry out the requirements of their jobs. Write a description of your job. Include the typical things that would be listed if an employer were advertising this position, but also include those things God is doing through you and the people you are ministering to. Think about who your neighbor is in this situation. Some possibilities to consider are employer, co-workers, customers, subordinates, and auxiliary personnel. For instance, a nurse's job is to administer care to patients, which includes myriad duties that are vital and integral to his or her vocation. While he or she is involved in this, there is encouragement offered to the patient, the family of the patient, other nurses, doctors, other medical professionals, and support staff. Think about your job and how specifically you can love your neighbor, whether or not it involves praying with or sharing God's love and redemption with him or her.

TELL THE TRUTH

Read 1 Kings 22:1–40.

Scrolling through social media, I came across a post from my friend Susan. She often posts interesting comments or links, so I paused to see what she had to say:

> We won't be hearing about this on CNN, MSNBC, or any of the other "news" sources so I'm taking it upon myself to share this here.

> I still don't care for the man personally, but when someone you don't care for is lied about and vilified far beyond what's already there and true, he has actually become a sympathetic figure (sort of) in my mind. Go figure.

> At any rate, here's some actual truth about this [politician] for a change.

Susan has a very strong political voice. In this instance, she felt a need to shed light on what was going on with a politician who wasn't one of her favorite people, but she felt she could help spread the truth.

Susan is not afraid to go head-to-head with anyone. If she sees something false, she feels a need to correct it. And if she sees some truth, she calls attention to it. She's been known to write letters to the editor, especially in response to falsehoods. She once taught a young adult Sunday School class about what the Bible has to say about some of the political issues of the time. She seeks out the truth and can't keep her mouth closed when she sees injustice or falsehood.

Another thing I am likely to see on Susan's page are statements that testify to her faith in Jesus Christ. She posts Scripture verses that are meaningful to her, links to Christian songs, information about goings-on at church, and articles in which someone's faith shone through the darkness.

Micaiah was another guy who needed to speak the truth. When he was summoned before Ahab, one of the vilest kings in Israel's history, he was warned beforehand that all the other four hundred prophets told the kings of Israel and Judah what they wanted to hear. "Agree with them" was the advice he heard. But Micaiah said he would have to say what God told him to say. He would have to tell the truth. The amazing thing about this story is that the kings asked for truth but couldn't accept it when it was presented. They still went ahead with their plans as if Micaiah hadn't told them what would happen. You would think that Ahab would have at least had second thoughts about riding to his death. I wonder what the point was of Jehoshaphat asking for a prophet of the Lord if he was going to ignore him. Micaiah told the truth whether it was popular or not. In this case, it definitely was not politically correct. Not only did he speak against the king, but he offended at least one of the other prophets. Life would have been easier for Micaiah if he would have just gone with the flow and said the same thing everyone else did. But that was not what God called him to do.

We need people who are willing to say what isn't popular to say, especially those who seek the Lord and seek truth. Bible-believing Christians can be involved in all areas of politics and stand up for what is right. Political vocations exist at many levels: national, state, and local. Some people don't run for office but are active in the campaigns of others or for certain causes. There is an urgency for lawyers who will take on cases to fight for what is right, as well as for people who write letters to bring about change or to keep undesirable changes from occurring.

In Luther's explanation of the Eighth Commandment, he says, "We should fear and love God so that we do not tell lies about our neighbor, betray him, slander him, or hurt his reputation, but defend him, speak well of him, and explain everything in the kindest way" (SC, explanation of the Eighth Commandment). Hmm. That's interesting. It is not just about refraining from lying; we should also speak up, tell the truth, and protect our neighbor.

Susan and other people I know enjoy researching issues, following political figures' careers, and sharing information with the hope of making change in our society. You may speak the truth like Micaiah. If people don't want to hear the truth, they won't. Just like the kings who summoned Micaiah, they will hear the words, but they won't accept them. You need to speak the truth anyway, even if no one will hear what you are saying. Micaiah's final words in the Bible were "Hear, all you peoples!" (1 Kings 22:28). Speak the truth!

1. John tells the story of another man who wasn't afraid to go head-to-head with the political leaders. In this case, it was the Pharisees. Read John 9. What were the Pharisees having an issue with?

2. The blind man, actually the former blind man, had to give his testimony over and over. The Pharisees didn't want to hear it, so they kept asking him to tell it again; presumably they thought that his message might change. How many times did he give his testimony?

3. Twice when the former blind man was being questioned, he had the opportunity to make a confession about who Jesus is. What did he say in John 9:17 and 30–33?

4. The man was not afraid to testify to the truth. His parents were more careful. What was their answer, and what was the reason for their ambiguity (vv. 20–21)?

5. His parents were afraid of the repercussions of speaking the truth. The man probably knew the repercussions also, but he told the truth anyway. What was the result of his statement, both immediately and a little later?

6. Read John 8:31–32. How do we know the truth?

7. According to John 14:16–17, why did King Ahab, King Jehoshaphat, and the Pharisees not believe the truth when it was presented to them clearly?

Journal Prompt

Is God calling you to a life in politics? Maybe you will be president of the United States of America. Maybe your role is to testify to the truth in a public forum. Explore in your journal writing how you could speak the truth. You could tell the Word of God to others, like the prophet Micaiah. You could tell what God has done in your life, like the man who was born blind. You could write letters or blogs or posts that declare the truth. You could teach a class that seeks out the truth. Read Psalm 25:4–5 and incorporate it into your journal entry somewhere.

KEEP SAYING YES

Read Matthew 1:18–2:23.

Kristin sat at her computer, trying to draft an email to send to her husband. Since he was on a short-term mission trip to Ethiopia, this was the only way to contact him, and she really needed to talk to him.

> You know how I have been volunteering with that organization that rescues girls from sex trafficking. Do you remember me telling you about Aliyah, the young woman that is pregnant? Well she's going to have to spend some time in jail. The baby is supposed to be born about five weeks before she is supposed to be released. Since we have already been approved with Safe Families, we have been asked to take the baby until Aliyah is released. I know this is huge but I feel like we should err on the side of love.

Scott hesitantly agreed. He did not want to fall in love with this child and then have to let her go. But he knew his wife's heart and how her heart would be broken if she couldn't help this mom and baby. It was temporary. Scott and Kristin made sure everyone understood that this baby would be with them for only five weeks. Besides, they already had four children, and they lived in a three-bedroom house. Their three girls shared the master bedroom. Their son had a room of his own, and Scott and Kristin shared one of the smaller rooms.

Chloe was only three days old when Kristin brought her home from the hospital. She was beautiful and the whole family fell in love with her.

The five weeks went way too fast. They got a phone call: Aliyah was out of jail and wanted her baby back. So, as had been arranged, Scott and Kristin met a lawyer in a discount department store parking lot in East L.A. They gave Chloe to the lawyer, who would then give her to her mom.

Safe Families is not quite foster care. Child Protective Services is not involved. This is a voluntary situation. When a family needs help, as in Aliyah's case with an incarceration, a family is found to take the children until their family can resume their responsibilities. But as soon as the family wants the children back, they are returned.

Kristin waited about a month and then reached out to Aliyah and offered to give her a break by keeping Chloe for a few days. Aliyah liked that idea and let Chloe stay for about ten days. This happened a couple of times.

Then Kristin learned that Aliyah had returned to her old life. Eventually the authorities were alerted that Chloe was in an unsafe situation. When Chloe returned to Kristin and Scott's home, it was through the foster care system. The next months were filled with court dates, visits, relatives seeking custody, and caring for an infant.

Scott might have tried to not fall in love with Chloe, but he was unsuccessful. And when Chloe came up for adoption, the whole family was ready to make her a permanent member of the family. They were still a big family in a little house, but Kristin prayed: "Heavenly Father, we will keep saying yes, but it would be wonderful if You could give us a bigger house." Soon, not only did a five-bedroom home come available to them, but it was perfect in so many ways.

This family brought a little bundle home for a five-week stay. They kept saying yes to whatever God put before them and they kept loving this sweet little girl through all the craziness. Within a year and a half, the adoption was final. God blessed this family with another family member and blessed this little girl with a stable and loving home.

In our Bible story today, we read about someone else who kept saying yes. Joseph is a sort of foster father to Jesus. Let's look at the things Joseph dealt with.

First, his fiancée told him she was already pregnant. That had to be tough to accept. He could have had her stoned, but he didn't want that. He was planning to quietly end their relationship, but through an angel who spoke to Joseph in a dream, God said for Joseph to take Mary as his wife and to raise this child and care for Him as his own. Joseph said yes and made sure that she remained a virgin until the child was born.

We know from Luke 2 that Joseph and Mary traveled to Bethlehem and slept in a stable. Then, after the child was born, again speaking through an angel who spoke to Joseph in a dream, God told Joseph to take his wife and child and flee to Egypt so the child wouldn't be killed (Matthew 2:13–15). And Joseph said yes and moved to Egypt, where his family stayed until God told him the threat was gone.

We see the family again in Luke 2:41–52, when Joseph and Mary frantically searched for their twelve-year-old son, only to find Him in the temple.

The Bible doesn't tell us much more about Joseph's relationship with Jesus, but we know Joseph was there day in and day out, being a parent to Jesus. Joseph was very much a part of raising this boy. He was called by God to raise the Son of God. It wasn't a convenient thing at all, but Joseph responded and trusted God and got to raise the Savior of the world.

And that's where our own adoption story begins. Through the sacrament that this foster child of Joseph instituted—Baptism— we are adopted into God's family. When we are baptized in the name of the triune God, we are made God's children, and He gives us faith, forgiveness, salvation, and eternal life with Him. Just like the children who enter a family by adoption, guardianship, foster care, or other means, we are part of the household, part of God's family. He treats us all the same—with love and mercy and grace.

"Repent and be baptized every one of you in the name of Jesus Christ for the forgiveness of your sins, and you will receive the gift of the Holy Spirit. For the promise is for you and for your children and for all who are far off, everyone whom the Lord our God calls to Himself." (Acts 2:38–39)

When I interviewed Kristin, I commented that hers was such an amazing story. She said, "It is an amazing story, and I can't believe we get to be a part of it." Awesome things can happen when you say yes to God, when you are open to Him leading you into difficult places.

1. How does James 1:27 describe pure religion?

Foster care, adoption, and the variety of ways you can care for and raise a child you did not give birth to are quite a bit more involved than "visiting orphans and widows in their affliction." Not everyone is called to serve in this way. It is my experience that those who are called get to experience an increased understanding of their need to rely on God. Many times, as my family has been involved in caring for others, I have thought that this job is more than I could handle. Each time, it isn't until I give the situation to God in prayer that I am able to deal with what is before me.

Read the prayer in Ephesians 3:14–21. This is a beautiful prayer for everyone, but as a foster parent, I find it to be empowering.

2. Write out all the blessings you find in this prayer.

3. Read 2 Samuel 9. David also reached out to an orphan. Mephibosheth was an adult but still benefited from the kindness of the king. Why did David want to show kindness to Mephibosheth? (See also 1 Samuel 20:14–15.)

4. Twice in this chapter, Mephibosheth is described in the same way. What is the one description we know about Mephibosheth?

5. See 2 Samuel 4:4. Why was Mephibosheth lame? Why do you think the nurse chose this action?

6. David was king. Mephibosheth was grandson to Saul, the former king, and Mica was the great-grandson of Saul. Contrast David's actions toward the royal descendants with those of Jehoram, another king of Judah. (See 2 Chronicles 21:4.)

Journal Prompt

Taking care of a child is a tremendous undertaking. Taking care of a child who was not born to you adds another level of effort. Not everyone is called to foster care or adoption, so even if you are not, there are many ways you can "visit orphans." Write in your journal about ways you might be able to say yes to God in this way. Google "Safe Families" and see how it is different from foster care. Look at different kinds of adoption (private adoption, foreign adoption, special needs adoption, and foster to adopt). Consider the various types of foster care. Some people do emergency foster care, which is where Chloe went for one night before she went to live with Kristen and Scott. This is a place for a child to be safe until social workers can arrange a placement. There is respite care, taking a child for a couple of days so the regular foster parents can have a break. You could be a big brother or big sister, either with the organization or if you know a family with that need. You may not want to get involved because you anticipate difficulty letting go when it's time for the child to return home. If that is the case, use this journal time to talk to God about that. There are many ideas to think about; don't try to address them all. Just start writing and see where God leads you.

PRAY FOR YOU

Read 2 Kings 18:13–19:37.

Grandma's house was filled with people. We don't visit Missouri very often because we live far away. So when we do, relatives come from all over the state for a reunion. There was lots of talking, laughing, eating, and having fun. Uncle Warren was trying to talk someone into going with him to get some chicken livers from the deli. Aunt Nancy was fawning over my three-year-old daughter. And Uncle Cliff always had a joke or story at the ready.

Then, without warning, Uncle Cliff quietly asked, "How can I pray for you?" I was surprised. I didn't know that I looked like I needed prayer. But I did need prayer. I was holding something close to my heart that I hadn't intended to share. But here he was, asking. And he was willing to pray for me. So we talked. I told him about my strained relationship with my parents. And I asked him how best to honor them despite the hurtful things they were doing and saying. Not only did he promise to pray for me, but he listened. He shared my burden, and he offered his wisdom, experience, and some things to read.

I thought about this question quite a bit afterward. It's a wonderful icebreaker. Even if he knew nothing about me, he could ask this question and potentially minister to me. Even if I weren't a Christian, this question opens the door to talking about God. But as a Christian, I could share my burden with a brother in Christ.

How often can we say we don't need prayer? We may not be actively thinking about it all the time. But if we give it any bit of thought, we can all come up with at least one area where we would appreciate some extra prayer.

By asking the question, my uncle made himself available to me. He continued to minister by praying for me and about my concerns. His simple question was all it took to move the conversation to a deeper place—a place where he could minister.

> Is anyone among you suffering? Let him pray. Is anyone cheerful? Let him sing praise. Is anyone among you sick? Let him call for the elders of the church, and let them pray over him, anointing him with oil in the name of the Lord. And the prayer of faith will save the one who is sick, and the Lord will raise him up. And if he has committed sins, he will be forgiven. Therefore, confess your sins to one another and pray for one another, that you may be healed. The prayer of a righteous person has great power as it is working. (James 5:13–16)

We see in our Bible reading how powerful our God is and how potent our prayers can be. The first thing Hezekiah did when he heard the threats of Sennacherib was go to God. He went to the house of the Lord and sent his servants to Isaiah to ask him to pray. Hezekiah prayed and asked for prayer, and God delivered in a mighty way. He sent an angel to kill the Assyrian troops. In one night, the angel killed 185,000 men. And the king, who thought he was more powerful than the living God, returned to his home to be struck down by his own sons.

Prayer is a mighty tool. We can, like Uncle Cliff, offer this gift to other people. We pray and let God defeat the enemies.

1. Read James 5:13–16. There is much to consider in this passage, but basically, we are looking at the fact that James tells us to go to God in all situations. How does he conclude this section? What is the last sentence of this passage? How does that apply to what we have been talking about?

2. What does Philippians 4:6 tell us about prayer? What does this say about the power of prayer?

3. Read 1 Timothy 2:1–4. What does Paul say is pleasing to God?

4. What is Paul doing in 2 Thessalonians 3:1–2? What does it look like?

5. When praying for people, we may or may not have all the details. That shouldn't stop us from praying. How is Romans 8:26–27 an encouragement to us in our prayer life?

6. My favorites of Paul's prayers were when he was praying for the people he was writing to. Paul frequently wrote a prayer in his letters. Read Philippians 1:9–11. A powerful way to pray is to pray Scripture. Take this passage and use its words to turn it into a prayer for someone you want to pray for.

Journal Prompt

"How can I pray for you?" Could you inject this phrase into your conversations? Whom could you ask? Make a list of people you might be able to ask. If someone asked you how he could pray for you, would you have an answer? How would you want someone to pray for you?

Called to the World, Near and Far

Jerusalem, Judea, Samaria, and the end of the earth. Wow! What does that mean to me? Little me, living here in twenty-first-century United States? That was a pretty tall and exciting order to the disciples in Jesus' day. Jerusalem. That's where the disciples were when Jesus said these words. He was telling them they needed to tell people they knew and saw everyday about Him. Judea. That was a bigger area that encompassed Jerusalem. So, they needed to spread out, but still they were telling the people relatively close to them. Samaria. Oh! We've read about how they felt about the Samaritans. They were expected to go to the less desirable people and share the love of Jesus with them. And to the end of the earth? That's a long way! But some of those disciples took Jesus' words to heart and went a long way. And God provided the means for getting there. This week, we are going to look at how we can be Jesus' witnesses nearby and to the end of the earth.

Memory Verse: "But you will receive power when the Holy Spirit has come upon you, and you will be my witnesses in Jerusalem and in all Judea and Samaria, and to the end of the earth." Acts 1:8

DAY 1

YOU DON'T HAVE TO GET A PASSPORT, BUT YOU CAN

Read Acts 17:16–34.

You don't have to get a passport or go abroad to make a difference in people's eternal lives. But you can. You don't have to cross an ocean to share God's love with people; but if you do, it makes an impression. I used to think there wasn't much value in short-term mission projects. I felt that to really make a difference, you needed to spend enough time to develop relationships, so you were better off going for years or trying to minister close to home. There are people in our own area that need to hear about the love of God.

But then my son Nick spent a semester abroad when he was in college. He went to ten countries; and besides working on academics, the group he was with worked with missionaries and completed service projects.

When Nick got home, we had a lot to talk about. One of our first conversations was about his time in Vietnam. "You were doing shots?"

"They were rice wine shots; it was a cultural thing."

"But you are not twenty-one yet!" My voice was a high-pitched, judgmental, mom voice.

"There is no minimum drinking age in Vietnam. As I was saying, they were rice wine shots, and they were provided to us by communist officials. They were an important cultural part of a special meal served to us by the local communist officials, and refusing would have been rude." Nick had this calm, instructive tone in his voice.

I breathed out audibly. I didn't really have anything more to say.

"Mom, let me tell you what Chinh, the communist official, told us."

"Okay." I was glad to move on to a different topic.

"He told us those guys out there in the rice paddies, they think we are here for one of three reasons. No one would come so far to help people they don't know unless it was for one of these reasons. First, that we are crazy. Second, we are CIA and the government sent us to spy on them."

I chuckled. "The CIA?"

"Yeah. The third is that we have come because of religion."

"Which you did. You were working with the missionary from Lutheran Church—Missouri Synod World Missions. You built a drainage ditch for their community center."

"Yes. Chinh said that he knows they think like that because that is how he used to think. People would come over claiming to be on a mission trip and it was because of their God. And so he decided he should read the Bible. He read the whole Bible and because of that, he became a Christian. Not only him, but his entire family."

Nick was awed by Chinh's testimony. A whole family, a whole communist family, became Christian because some people took the time to go to Vietnam on a short-term mission trip. Those people probably don't even know the impact that they had. Nick and his classmates knew that the drainage ditch they worked on would benefit the people and help the long-term missionary with his work. But they would never know if God used their presence there to lead the people to faith in Him.

> And this gospel of the kingdom will be proclaimed
>
> throughout the whole world as a testimony to all nations,
>
> and then the end will come. (Matthew 24:14)

Once Paul became a Christian, his life became a series of short-term mission projects. Nick stayed in each country for about two weeks. Paul stayed some places for years. Other times, his stay in a place was brief. The duration of his mission trips was determined by how long it took to accomplish what God wanted done.

Paul visited Athens, a city whose inhabitants were known for philosophical interest and desire for new information. Paul engaged not only Jews in the synagogue, as was his custom, but philosophers and intellectuals in the marketplace. Paul was educated and intelligent enough to relate to the Greeks on their level; and that's what he did. He stepped into their culture and filled in the empty places by sharing the Gospel and the story of Christ's resurrection with them. Not all were ready to accept this strange new thought. However, some did. What a life-changing experience for Dionysius and Damaris.

1. Does Acts 17:16–34 record Paul quoting the Scriptures in his address to the Athenians? If not, what does he quote? What thoughts do you have about why this might have been more effective?

2. How can you apply this approach when speaking with non-Christians?

3. What object did Paul use to start his presentation and how did he use it?

4. Read 1 Corinthians 9:22 and 10:31–33. What do these passages say about bringing the Gospel to other cultures? How did you see these verses acted out in the story of Nick and also the story of Paul?

5. Though there are plenty of people around us with whom we can share the Gospel, what does Jesus say in Matthew 28:19–20?

6. Isaiah 6:8 can help us with our response. What does Isaiah say when God calls? What do we learn later in Isaiah 52:7?

Journal Prompt

Whom can you tell, "Your God reigns!"? To whom can you proclaim salvation? How beautiful are your feet? In your journal today, ask God where He is calling you to. Pray and ask God if He wants you to go abroad or to a different region of the United States. Today we discussed engaging other cultures. You can probably find ways of doing that without leaving town. Ask God if He is calling you to minister to a different culture closer to home. Then see if you can conclude your prayer honestly with "Here am I! Send me."

I'M SOMEBODY

Read John 13:1–17.

"I'm going to go for a five-gallon walk," my friend Nick has been known to say. Five-gallon walk? What is he talking about? Distance can be measured by various means but not gallons. Nick takes his five-gallon bucket, small dustpan, broom, and a grappler and walks the neighborhood, picking up trash until he fills his bucket. Unfortunately, a five-gallon walk is usually only a couple of blocks. He has a bigger trash can in the back of his truck so he can dump his bucket and go out again. He usually spends about an hour three times per week picking up other people's trash.

I asked how he got started doing this. He told me there was a lot of trash in his neighborhood. He hates trash; it drives him crazy. *Somebody should do something about this,* he thought. Then he realized, *I'm somebody.* So he got some professional equipment and started picking up trash. People in the neighborhood started honking and waving, and the area began to look nicer.

Then he wondered, *How can I make this a witnessing opportunity?* He had the idea of wearing a safety vest with Scripture on it. Nick paraphrased Ephesians 6:7–8 and had "Serve as for Jesus" put on the vest. Then, not only was he helping his neighbors, he was sharing with them the reason behind his actions. He has had opportunities to witness to people when he is out and wearing his vest. One man walked up, read the vest, and said, "Jesus? All right!"

And let us not grow weary of doing good, for in due season

we will reap, if we do not give up. (Galatians 6:9)

Then a local television station interviewed him. After getting footage of him at work, they asked him why he did this. He thought, *I'm just going to say this,* so he answered, "If my Lord and Savior, Jesus Christ, can wash His disciples' feet, I can pick up some trash in the neighborhood." They left it in and aired it.

Jesus did even dirtier work for us. The Son of God humbled Himself and left the perfection of heaven to take on human form and be our servant. He cleaned up our mess and made us clean. This action takes place when we are baptized by "a lavish washing away of sin" (*LSB*, p. 269).

Today we read about Jesus washing His disciples' feet. What did He say when He was finished? "For I have given you an example, that you also should do just as I have done to you" (John 13:15). Jesus demonstrated how we are to love and serve our neighbor by performing one of the most menial of tasks. He got down on the ground and washed the dirty, stinky feet of men who walked everywhere. He showed us that we are not too good to love others.

1. What does John say in 13:3 that Jesus knew about Himself as He got up to serve the disciples by washing their feet?

2. This seemed like an incredible act for Jesus, the teacher, to stoop down and wash the dirty feet of His students. But what did He do for them the next day that was even more beneath Him? Read John 19:16–18.

3. Read Matthew 20:25–28. What does Jesus say we need to do to be great? What does He say is the reason He came?

4. Read Philippians 2:1–11. What does verse 5 say about Christ Jesus? What do the following verses say He did about it? What will come of His actions? What does Paul challenge us to do at the beginning of this passage?

5. We can't do a study on loving our neighbor without reading the story of the Good Samaritan. Read Luke 10:25–37. What did Jesus say when the lawyer asked Him what He should do to inherit eternal life?

6. Jesus told a story about who our neighbor is. Based on His story, name some neighbors that you might not normally think of as neighbors.

7. What is Jesus' definition of a neighbor? See verses 36 and 37.

8. What does Jesus tell the lawyer—and us—to do?

Journal Prompt

Nick served his neighbors by picking up trash. I know of a couple who, when they moved into a new neighborhood, left notes on the neighbors' doors offering to help in whatever way they needed, like bringing in garbage containers, sharing cookies at Christmas, helping with yard work, just being neighborly. These actions led to an expanded ministry. What could you do to serve people in your neighborhood? Is there a need you can help with? If you don't know your neighbors, what could you do to meet them? Conversely, have you received help from any of your neighbors? If someone asks how they could help you, how would you answer?

TO THE END OF THE EARTH

Read Philippians 4:10–20.

John and Missy live in Scotland with their three children. They used to live in California and go to the same church my family attends. Missy even babysat for my children when they were younger. They used to live here, but they sold everything they had and moved to Scotland to be missionaries. Now one of their vocations is sharing the love of Jesus with people who have rejected the Church. They are engaged in a one-on-one ministry, developing relationships and sharing with their new friends and acquaintances about what God means to them.

I saw Missy recently. She was back home raising money for visas so they can remain in Scotland. You see, their ministry is fully funded by donations. They have to find people willing to support their ministry for it to continue. One of the exciting parts of John and Missy getting support this way is that we have the opportunity to answer God's call to be His witness "to the end of the earth" without having to sell everything and move like they did. We can contribute financially to people who are willing to be there. They wouldn't be able to do the things they do and reach the people they are reaching without the support from people back home.

Becca spent a semester abroad in Ghana. While there, she and a friend became deeply concerned about what the children and young women had to do to survive. They came up with a plan for a nonprofit organization to help them. Water is sold in plastic packets. Once the water is gone, the packets litter the streets everywhere. Becca and her friend took this trash, cleaned it, and sewed it into purses and bags. She taught women there to make these items, and the women were able to make a product and an income. Then she taught them how to batik cloth and added this to the purses. A project like this needs people in place to facilitate its progress, and it needs capital to get it started. Now, it has been turned over to the locals to run, and it is an international organization.

As we discussed, a short-term mission trip is one way for people to minister to the end of the earth. But even if you are not ready to pack your bag, you can have an influence. You can help someone you know go abroad and share the love of Jesus. When my children first started to go on mission trips, I resisted sending out a support letter. But my daughter told me that doing so would give people an opportunity to partner with her in spreading the Gospel.

Providing financial support to missionaries is not the only way we can witness to the end of the earth without physically going there. We can join national and international organizations that are using local people to spread the Gospel and to reach out to those in need at home and all over the world through specific mission ministries. You could even start your own ministry if you feel led to do that.

In the passage we read today, Paul is thanking the Philippians for the gift they sent. This wasn't the first time they had provided for his needs. The Philippians were supporting Paul in his missionary work. In 2 Corinthians 11:9, Paul writes: "And when I was with you and was in need, I did not burden anyone, for the brothers who came from Macedonia supplied my need." Paul was supported in his missionary work by multiple congregations. We can be a part of reaching to the end of the earth by financially supporting people and agencies that are at the end of the earth.

1. In the lesson for today, Paul doesn't seem to be concerned about money. What was of more value to him than money?

2. How does Paul describe the gift the Philippians gave him in verse 18?

3. What else does Paul say is a fragrant offering and a sacrifice in Ephesians 5:2?

4. In Philippians 4:19, what blessing does Paul say will come from their sacrifice?

5. Romans 15:22–33 is like a support letter from Paul to the Romans. He tells them what he intends to do and asks for their help in accomplishing it. He alludes to their previous financial help in the beginning and shows them how others have risen up to help those in need. But what does he ask for directly? In other words, what does he most desire from them?

6. Read 1 Timothy 5:17–18. What does Paul say in reference to what we are studying today? What does the analogy of the ox mean? (Paul also quotes this law in 1 Corinthians 9:8–12.) What does Paul come right out and say in verse 18?

My friend Mary Lou told me that when she and her husband were in the mission field in Africa, what benefited her most was encouragement from the people back home. When they were in Africa, her husband received a salary from the church's mission board. They didn't have to raise their own support or depend on contributions from regular donors as many missionaries must today. But they appreciated the encouragement, prayers, and occasional financial gifts from home.

Journal Prompt

Write a prayer asking God how you can be His witness to the end of the earth. Some of the things we have considered in this lesson are financially supporting a mission organization or missionary (long-term or short-term), going on a mission (long-term or short-term), praying for missionaries and the people they are reaching, and otherwise encouraging missionaries. Talk to God about some of these options or others. How is He leading you to witness your faith in Him?

LUNCH WITH JESUS

Read Matthew 25:34–40.

Bethany had just gotten off work and was headed home. As she drove, she saw a young man sitting in front of an old abandoned theater. He was holding a sign asking for help. Bethany was struck by how young he looked. He couldn't be any older than she was, and she was just twenty-two. She pulled up next to him, rolled down her window, and asked, "Is there something you would like from Jack in the Box?" He made his request and Bethany drove off to place the order.

When Bethany returned, she handed him a bag and asked, "Can I join you?"

He shrugged and nodded to the ample space on the sidewalk.

"My name is Bethany."

"I'm Robert."

"Oh, that's my boyfriend's name, so it will be easy to remember." Bethany sat on the concrete and got her burger out of the bag. "So, Robert, tell me about yourself."

Robert bit into his burger and seemed to think about what he was going to say. He told Bethany about his life and what had brought him to this point. There were things Bethany could tell he didn't really want to talk about. Some things he told her anyway. He told her he had grown up in many foster homes. He told her that initially he had been placed with his siblings, but then they were separated. At times, their foster parents worked to help them see each other, but not always.

Bethany's heart went out to this young man. She suggested that he check out the Rescue Mission. He said he had been there before and didn't want to go back. But she urged him and even gave him bus fare. Before Bethany left, she prayed with Robert.

Wow! It is challenge enough for many of us to give money to someone who has a hand out, but Bethany gave this stranger more than money. She gave him lunch and her time. She listened to his story and showed him compassion. Our Bible lesson today says that what we do for the "least of these," we do for Jesus. So taking that one step further, Bethany had lunch with Jesus. I want to have lunch with Jesus, but I'm not sure if I have as much nerve as Bethany. I don't know if I would have the courage to invite "Jesus" to eat with me.

Bethany's training started at home. Her mother would buy gift cards and keep them in her car. Then, when she came across someone asking for food, she could find a card that matched a fast food restaurant nearby and give it to them. Then they would be less likely to misuse it, and she wouldn't be leaving them hungry.

> As each has received a gift, use it to serve one another, as
> good stewards of God's varied grace: whoever speaks, as
> one who speaks oracles of God; whoever serves, as one
> who serves by the strength that God supplies—in order that
> in everything God may be glorified through Jesus Christ.
> To Him belong glory and dominion forever and ever. Amen.
> (1 Peter 4:10–11)

This form of assistance would be easier for me, but then I wouldn't have the blessing of having lunch with Jesus. (Well, at least not this way.) God calls us all to different ministries. If God calls me to eat lunch with strangers, He will also give me what I need to do it, including courage. But God may call me to eat lunch with Him in a different way, which I believe He has.

1. According to Matthew 25:34–40, what are some things we can do for Jesus when we reach out and help "the least of these" around us?

2. Read Proverbs 19:17. What is the action verb used in this verse that shows what we are doing for the Lord when we are generous with the poor? What will God do in response?

3. Think about that for a minute. How are giving to the poor and lending to God different? How are they the same? Does this verse have any impact on your attitude about giving to the poor? Is God a trustworthy credit risk?

4. Read Isaiah 58:6–8. In these verses, God contrasts a traditional fast with a focus on things that matter. According to these verses, what kinds of things does God ask us to do that demonstrate our love for Him?

5. What imagery is in Isaiah 58:10, and what benefit is there to honoring God's desire here?

6. James is much more straightforward in his language and expectations. What is the attitude conveyed in James 2:15–16?

Journal Prompt

Bethany told me she feels that if we give money to someone, then it is between that person and God what he or she does with it. She is allowing God to use her, and she is trusting God to take care of how the helping happens. Bethany said, "So what if people take advantage of us?" What does your personal ministry look like for reaching out to the poor? Could you, like Bethany, buy a stranger lunch and sit down and share a meal with him? Do you feel more comfortable with her mom's practice of handing out gift cards? Are you okay with handing out money? Would you prefer to work through an agency that screens applicants? Record your thoughts and resolve to make a plan.

ACROSS THE TRACKS

Read Matthew 18:1–14.

I sat at a little table with three kindergartners. Each of us had scissors in one hand and a square of colored paper in the other. "First you cut off two corners," I instructed, and I proceeded to demonstrate. The little hands worked to follow my example. "Now we cut off these points to make our corners more rounded."

As they worked, Latisha said, "I wrote lmmmmr this weekend."

"You wrote what?" I asked.

"Mmrmmr."

I was baffled. But for some reason, telling me this seemed important to her. So I took a deep breath and asked her to tell me one more time what she wrote.

It was her turn to take a deep breath, obviously a little exasperated with me. Then, very clearly, she explained, "When your dad is in jail, you write a letter."

"Oh," I said. First the meaning of her words hit me and then the comprehension of what she was saying hit me. Then I felt a heaviness in my heart for this sweet little girl. "So you wrote a letter to your dad?" I asked.

"Uh-huh," she nodded.

I volunteered twice a week in this kindergarten classroom. Latisha was by no means the only needy child in that class. In fact, had she not volunteered the information that she did, I would not have suspected anything out of the ordinary in her life. Justin, for example, was more hungry for attention. He always seemed to look forward to coming to my table to work. Then Justin disappeared, and I didn't see him for several weeks. When he came back, his hair, which had been past his shoulders, was buzzed. I suspected he had been dealing with lice.

The kids and the teacher said they looked forward to my visits. Before I started homeschooling, I volunteered in my children's classrooms. I often wondered how valuable my services were. Oh, of course my children looked forward to me coming in. But there were always so many parents and grandparents volunteering that the actual need for my being there was questionable.

But in this classroom, in a neighborhood farther from home, I was the only volunteer. The teacher said that if it hadn't been for me, these kids would not have had the opportunity to do much art at all.

Over the months, the students grew accustomed to me and occasionally gave me glimpses into their personal lives. I began to realize how much my volunteer work in this public school classroom was a ministry. One that required little of me. I showed up at the designated time and performed the simple tasks the teacher laid out for me. In the meantime, I had a reason to be involved in these young people's lives.

Jesus talks in today's lesson about how precious children are to Him. He tells us what a blessing it is to love on them and to do our best for them. He loves each one of us, not because of great things, or even selfless things we have done, but because of the great thing He did for us.

In that public-school classroom, I couldn't talk about Jesus' love for them or how He paid the price for all their sins so they could live with Him forever. But I could show them Jesus' love. I could treat them like they are valuable. I could look for God's lost sheep.

Typically, our questions have been about how we can minister. How we can reach out to others. How we can do something. And we will talk about that. But here, I want to rest in God's love so we don't get so caught up in serving that we forget that Jesus loves us so much that He died for us. We are to come to Him in the same way that young children in need come to a grown-up—with humility, trust, and confidence. We are Jesus' little lambs. When we stray, He seeks us out, and He searches relentlessly until we are safely back in His fold.

1. Read Zephaniah 3:17. The verse tells us that our mighty God is with us. What three things does it say He does? How does this make you feel?

2. Read Romans 5:8 and John 15:13. After reading these carefully back-to-back, close your Bible and write the message that God is giving you here. (The first verse was penned by Paul after Jesus died. The second is words Jesus spoke before His crucifixion.)

3. In our Bible reading for today, Jesus talks about what a shepherd would do for his sheep and says that that is how God feels about His people. Read the following passages about our Shepherd: Psalm 23; Isaiah 40:10–11. What does Jesus do for His sheep?

4. Jesus is our Good Shepherd. But sometimes He takes
    on a mask and asks us to tend His sheep, as He did with
    Peter (John 21). What does Acts 20:28 direct us to do?

5. Let's return to our Bible story. In Matthew 18:5, what does
    Jesus say we do when we receive one of His children in His
    name? By showing love to one of His children, what are we
    doing?

6. In Luke 12:32, what does Jesus tell us that God wants to
    give to His flock? What word in this verse captures the
    feeling of God's love for us?

Journal Prompt

So often when we think of mission work, we think of going across
the ocean. But can we go across the tracks? Is there someplace closer
where you could volunteer and be an ambassador for Jesus? Consider
the schools, hospitals, care facilities, or service organizations in your
town. Consider other institutions that may or may not be Christian but
where Christians can be involved. Brainstorm some ideas, then write
about how one of the opportunities might work in your life.

Called to Embrace Your Passions

What is your passion? What do you enjoy? How can your desires help you share Jesus' love and witness to your faith in Him with others? That is what we get to explore this week. We will see how other people have turned their passions into ministry opportunities. Ministry can be fun, exciting, and fulfilling. Colossians 3:17 lets us know that whatever we do can be done to the glory of God.

Memory Verse: "And whatever you do, in word or deed, do everything in the name of the Lord Jesus, giving thanks to God the Father through Him." Colossians 3:17

DAY 1

FUN SPORTS

Read Acts 4:1–22.

It was a crisp Saturday morning and the school athletic field was filled with about a hundred young children wearing various colors of the same T-shirt that served as their uniform. The children were there to play soccer. And there were probably four times as many spectators gathered on that same field. Christian music was playing over loudspeakers as the children warmed up and parents and grandparents set up chairs along the sidelines. The music stopped, and a man's voice came over the loudspeaker: "Please rise for the National Anthem." After the National Anthem, John, the man behind the voice, read a Bible verse: "For all have sinned and fall short of the glory of God, and are justified by His grace as a gift, through the redemption that is in Christ Jesus" (Romans 3:23–24). He went on to explain a little bit about what that means: Even though we mess up, make mistakes, and can never be perfect, God loves us and has given us a gift of salvation. Jesus died on the cross so we could be reconciled to God and live forever with Him. John concluded with a prayer and then officially started the games.

This routine was repeated several times throughout the morning, each time with different teams and spectators. For six weeks there were games every Saturday morning, always with the Word of God being shared with everyone within range of the loudspeaker.

This sports league is John's vision. He started it fifteen years ago. John had been working as the CEO of another children's sporting association that was, by name, a Christian organization. However, every time he put any reference to Jesus in anything, there was pushback. One of the final straws was when the public schools refused to send the organization's fliers home with the students because of the mention of Jesus on the page. He took the situation to the organization's board of directors, where things got confrontational. John ended up walking away from his job. God had plans. John felt compelled to start his own league. He prayed and trusted that God would bless his efforts. It wasn't easy, but every time John came across a problem, there was a solution. John believes that God wanted him to do this.

Fifteen years later, FUN (Faith Unity Nurture) Sports is still going strong with more than a thousand young athletes playing each season. The best part is that John is able to share God's Word with these young people and their families. One grandmother told John, "This is the only church my grandchildren will ever experience. Their mom won't take them to church." Another woman asked if her husband could coach even though he doesn't go to church. John agreed even though originally his expectation was that coaches were Christians. By the end of the season, the woman reported that her husband had started attending worship services at a local church.

John's plan is simple: he uses his passion for children's sports to share the Word of God, and he trusts the Holy Spirit to do the rest.

In the Bible story, Peter and John annoyed the religious leaders because they were teaching the people about Christ's resurrection. When they were asked to explain themselves, Peter answered boldly and told them in no uncertain terms that even though the religious leaders had killed Jesus, God had raised Him from the dead. And the only way to salvation is through Jesus Christ.

Like my friend John, these apostles were passionate about their calling to share the Gospel, so they boldly spoke the truth about Jesus even when met with resistance.

1. Read Acts 4:19–20. When Peter and John were before the religious authorities, they were ordered not to teach or speak any more about Jesus. What was their answer? How would you say that in your own words?

2. After our reading, the story continues. They were released; then they went and told their friends about their experience. What did they pray for as recorded in Acts 4:29?

3. Read Acts 5:17–42. What was the result of the apostles continuing to speak about Jesus? What did Peter say in verse 29?

4. John started FUN Sports so the kids could enjoy sports in an environment where Jesus is welcome. Every week a Bible passage is shared with those in attendance. John told me sometimes he wonders if anyone really hears it. Nevertheless, he continues to share the Word of God and to trust that God is faithful to work faith in the hearts of those present. Read Isaiah 55:10–11. Based on this passage, what could you say to John to encourage him to continue sharing the Bible verses?

5. It was Paul's custom on the Sabbath to go to the synagogue to worship and to speak to the Jews. What does he do in Acts 16:13? What does it say God did here? How does this fit with the story we read about John and his FUN Sports?

Journal Prompt

"Whatever you do, work heartily, as for the Lord and not for men, knowing that from the Lord you will receive the inheritance as your reward" (Colossians 3:23–24). What things are you passionate about? How can you "work heartily" at them for the Lord? John is doing this as a full-time ministry; he doesn't get paid and he doesn't have another job. Not everyone can do that. But we could get involved with someone like John or with an organization like FUN Sports. He can't do everything by himself and is always in need of volunteers. Think about your hobbies and passions in the light of how they can be used to benefit others. Write a prayer and ask God if there is some way He is calling you to get involved that will glorify Him. And remember to ask God to help you speak boldly about His love for others.

DAY 2

REMEMBER

Read Joshua 3–4.

"Can I look at one of the scrapbooks?" My daughter, then nine, surveyed the shelf holding my albums. "Of course, Sweetie. Which one would you like to see?" I was thinking she was interested in the one that is all about her. Or maybe the one when she was born and baptized. Or the big water fight we had on Easter.

"One with words," Angela said.

"Hmm, yeah," I smiled. I hadn't gotten around to journaling in all of them. I select the photographs and tell myself, *I'll go back and write about that later.*

Angela felt a need to ease my conscience. "I like all of them, but reading the stories is fun." Even as a young child she was sensitive to people's feelings.

More recently, Tony has been enjoying the albums. He will sit and look at them and comment on what silly thing Mark was doing or how little Angela was. The sad thing is that I have gotten behind and there were no albums created since his birth. This realization motivated me, so I got a new scrapbook and started a Tony album. I have gotten to age five for him; he is thirteen, but at least it is something. I plan to have him help me get it caught up.

Scrapbooking is my hobby. I love family pictures, and I enjoy creating the pages to showcase special times in our lives. I am not only having fun; I am acting as a historian for my family. It is a way to remember events and people that are important to us. My friend Char says scrapbooks can be a legacy of faith—that is, an accounting of our faith and what is important to us for future generations. Char is a new grandma and has started a book for her granddaughter. She included a "fear not" page, and each time she comes across a Bible verse that talks about not fearing, she writes it in the book.

People in Bible times used stones to memorialize events. For example, the day Moses and the children of Israel crossed the Jordan River on dry land and entered into the Promised Land was one worth memorializing. If it had happened today, there would have been people with cameras documenting the event and a statue would have been erected.

God wanted them to remember that day particularly. He wanted them to remember what He did for them and what He gave them, so God had them collect twelve stones, one for each tribe, from the river bottom and carry them out to create a memorial.

Today, we can see at a glance what God has done for us. We have His Word, the Bible, in various formats—printed Bibles, audiobooks, digital books. The Bible memorializes past events of God's people so we can remember that God has delivered us from the wilderness of sin into the promised land of heaven.

> You yourselves like living stones are being built up as a
> spiritual house, to be a holy priesthood, to offer spiritual
> sacrifices acceptable to God through Jesus Christ. (1 Peter 2:5)

In Joshua 4:1–10, we see where Joshua stacked twelve stones taken from the place where the priests stood holding the ark of the covenant on the riverbed. This memorial was a remembrance for these people and for generations to come of what God had done for them. It is so important for us to remember the blessings God has given us, both big and little. When times get tough, as they sometimes do, it helps to be able to remember and see how God has always been with us and how He has provided for us.

1. The story we read today is not the only time stones were used to commemorate an event. Read Genesis 28:10–22. What was being remembered in this passage?

2. Besides using stones to remember special events, God's people celebrated holy days in remembrance. Read Exodus 12:25–27. What holiday is instituted here? What were the children of Israel celebrating? How is this celebration observed in our worship service today?

3. What holy day was instituted in Esther 9:20–32? What were they celebrating?

4. Examples of another form of remembrance are found in these passages. What kind of remembrance was this? And what was being remembered in each case?

    Exodus 15:1–18

    Judges 5

    Numbers 21:27–30

    2 Samuel 22

    1 Chronicles 16:8–36

    Luke 1:46–55

5. What theme runs through most of these occasions of remembrance?

6. What phrase did we come across several times in these passages? What does this suggest we should be mindful of? See Joshua 4:21; 12:26.

Journal Prompt

There are multiple ways we can praise God and remember His love, provision, and saving power. We talked about a few in this session. Here are more to spark your brainstorming. Along the idea of stacking rocks, a recent trend was leaving painted rocks for people to find, documenting the find in social media, and leaving the rocks in other locations. My husband and I tried a version of this. We planned to make a rock garden using rocks from our trips. So we picked up a rock, painted the date and place where we found it on it, and added it to our garden. We currently have two painted rocks and a bunch of random plain rocks that we didn't document so we have no idea where they came from. The idea was fun for us, though maybe you will be better at follow-through. My pastor writes in his Bible, recording his thoughts about verses as he studies. When he fills it up, he passes it to one of his children. What ways can you pass on to future generations what God has done for you and your family?

SHARING MY GIFTS

Read 1 Kings 6.

I pulled into the church parking lot and told Tony to look for a red truck. There were few vehicles in the parking lot that Saturday morning, but since our parking lot is in several sections, I wanted an extra pair of eyes.

"There it is." Tony pointed. There was the truck. Nearby, a tall thin man wearing cowboy boots and a cowboy hat was flying a little drone. As we got closer, we saw a bigger drone on the back of the truck. That's the reason we were here. My friend Howard was letting us see the drones and even fly them.

"This little drone is getting away from me," Howard called as soon as we were within earshot. "It's meant for flying inside; the wind is catching it." He put the little drone down and picked up the big one to get it ready to fly. He talked nonstop, telling us all about drones, how to fly them, the different ones he owns, and his plans to take the drone with him on the mission trip to Scotland. This is his passion, and I could tell from his enthusiasm.

My son's enthusiasm was not as overt. He looked pleased when Howard offered him the controls, but it wasn't until we got back in the car that he talked about it. It was clear that the experience was exciting for him.

Howard has been like that for as long as I have known him, which is a few decades. He loves to play, and he is excited about involving others in his passions. He may have had no idea what an amazing opportunity it was for this thirteen-year-old boy to get to play with such a sophisticated toy.

I met Howard when I was in high school. He was an adult volunteer and accompanied the youth group I was in on trips and outings. Though he is eleven years older than I am, he always seems young at heart. When my own kids were in high school, Howard was still involved with the youth. My sons were impressed that Howard had cool paintball equipment. He even had a paintball tank! He found ways to share his toys. He brought paintball markers on the men's fishing trip. He provided paintball equipment for a youth retreat activity. And when my son Mark was making a movie for the Christian Film Festival, Howard loaned him props.

Howard's interests extend beyond toys. He and his wife love to dance. They shared their passion with the congregation by taking an instrumental role in several dances. For example, at a sock hop, they brought a dance teacher to teach swing dancing. My older kids and their friends had a great time. Howard likes to have fun and he likes to share.

> Now there are varieties of gifts, but the same Spirit; and
>
> there are varieties of service, but the same Lord; and
>
> there are varieties of activities, but it is the same God who
>
> empowers them all in everyone. (1 Corinthians 12:4–6)

In the Bible story for today, we see Solomon using his resources to glorify God. He had great wealth and used that to build a magnificent temple for God. If we go back to 1 Kings 1, we see where Solomon got his riches—they were a gift from God. God was pleased with Solomon's request for wisdom, so He gave Solomon more than he asked for. He gave him the wisdom and knowledge but also incredible wealth and honor.

God gives us gifts, sometimes incredible gifts. We need to remember where such gifts came from, and we need to be willing to share. Solomon didn't forget that his riches were from God, and he gave back in the form of a wonderful temple to honor God. Howard has gifts from God; he has always been willing to give back and to honor God by sharing his gifts with others. How can we enjoy God's provisions to the glory of God?

WHEREVER LOVE MAY LEAD

1. Read James 1:7. What does James say that God gives us?

2. While there are a variety of gifts from God, today we focused on material gifts such as money and possessions. Read 1 Peter 4:7–11. In verse 10, what does Peter say we should do with our gifts?

3. The last part of that verse says, "as good stewards of God's varied grace." What does that mean?

4. Why should we serve one another with the gifts that God gives us?

5. What is the greatest gift God has given us? Why is it so wonderful?

6. Read Matthew 25:14–30. What does the master say in verses 21 and 23? What had these servants done to precipitate such a response?

Journal Prompt

God has given each of us many gifts—extravagant gifts, different gifts. He wants us to use His gifts to us to glorify Him, and He wants us to use them to love and serve one another. God's gifts to us can be categorized this way: time, talents, treasures. Usually when we talk about treasures, we are talking about giving money to the church. But our financial contribution—our tithe—is just part of what we can share. Think about the time, talents, and treasures God has given you. How can you share your gifts? Pray about what He has given you that He would like you to share. Ask Him who He wants you to share with. And ask Him how you can glorify Him with the gifts He has given you.

DAY 4

CUDDLE WITH ME

Read 1 Samuel 1:1–28.

Linda smiled as she looked at the newborn in her arms. For years, she had prayed, begging God to give her a child. After years of praying for a child, she changed her prayer. She asked God to take away her desire for children.

The little guy in her arms now was eating voraciously. *That's good,* she thought. *It will help him gain weight and grow stronger.* The baby finished his bottle of formula, and Linda moved him to her shoulder, patting him on the back, waiting for the burp. After she was done feeding and burping, she returned him to his bassinet, moved on to the next bed, and picked up another baby—this time, a little girl.

God didn't answer either of Linda's prayers the way she asked Him to. Instead, He let her know that He had another plan for her. He placed it on her heart to get involved in a volunteer program at the county hospital called the Cuddler Program. Linda headed up volunteers who came in regularly to hold, rock, and feed abandoned babies until they were placed in a foster home or were adopted. Linda was the Saturday cuddler for ten years. The emptiness she felt at not having children of her own gave her the desire to fill a void in the lives of these babies.

Hannah also desperately wanted children. She, too, laid her heart open to God. She promised God that if He gave her a son, she would give him back to God. Had she not experienced her time of barrenness, she would not have made this vow. God did give her the son she asked for. She, in turn, gave him back to God. Samuel grew up in the temple and became a great judge and prophet of God.

Sometimes, God uses our desires to bring about great things. Had Hannah been able to have children from the start, she would not have needed to ask God for help. She would not have made the promise that she did in her prayer. She would not have taken her young son to Eli to be raised in the temple. Our Creator used her faith and her barrenness for His purposes, and things were put in place so Samuel was in place to judge Israel.

If Linda had been able to have children, she would probably have been too busy taking care of them to work at a cuddler program. It was by satisfying her unmet need that she helped to meet the needs of others. God used her because of the desire she had for children.

> But God, being rich in mercy, because of the great love
> with which He loved us, even when we were dead in our
> trespasses, made us alive together with Christ—by grace
> you have been saved. (Ephesians 2:4–5)

It is frustrating to pray and pray about something and not get what we want from God. We may never know why He chooses to say no to us. But sometimes, perhaps years later, we can look back and see the wisdom of His decision. We may see how that unmet desire was a conduit for something greater than we could imagine. We may see how, if we had gotten what we asked for, we would have been limited in what we accomplished or even harmed. We may see that our unmet desires led to awesome ministry opportunities. God is amazing like that. We also may never see what God is doing in our lives, what purpose He has for letting our pain continue. I don't want to seem insensitive to the real hurt that people experience. After my second miscarriage, I was angry at God. I didn't understand. I habitually try to see how God is working in all things, but at that time I didn't feel God's love.

The truth is that we live in a world of sin, and this side of heaven we are going to experience pain, loss, and heartache. My goal here is not to deny the pain, but to look for what God accomplishes in spite of or because of that hurt.

Jeremiah 29:11 is a favorite Bible verse of many people. This is a verse of comfort, yet the context is as God's people were going into exile. They were forced out of their homes and country and most would not return. God was telling them that their lives would change, but that through it all He would still be with them. It reads: "For I know the plans I have for you, declares the LORD, plans for welfare and not for evil, to give you a future and a hope." These words assure us that in all things, whether we have whatever we want or not, God wants us to draw near to Him and to trust in His plans for us. That plan, ultimately, is that we live with Him forever in heaven. We can remember this each time we speak the words of the Apostles' Creed—"the communion of saints, the forgiveness of sins, the resurrection of the body, and the life everlasting" (*LSB*, p. 175).

1. Psalm 37:4 says, "Delight yourself in the LORD, and He will give you the desires of your heart." If He isn't giving what we ask for, what does that verse mean? Does that mean that we are not taking delight in Him? Or does it mean that what we ask for is not really the desire of our heart? Or will we find that God knows our heart more than we do and gives what it truly desires? What are your thoughts?

2. Read 2 Corinthians 12:7–10. What did Paul beg God for? Do you think Paul delighted in God? Did Paul get what he asked for?

3. What was God's response to Paul's request? Copy it from verse 9.

4. How does Paul sum up this exchange with God?

5. What is meant by these phrases: "My power is made perfect in weakness" and "when I am weak, then I am strong"?

Journal Prompt

Have you begged God for something only to get no as an answer? Tell about your request and go into detail about your desires. Then reflect on what the no answer has meant in your life. Did it give you opportunities you wouldn't have had? Did trying to satisfy that need help you to meet the needs of others? How did God's no draw you closer to Him and work faith in your heart?

DAY 5

COMRADES

Read Luke 1:5–56.

The man who got out of the car, Rick, didn't look like a typical hospice worker. He wore a T-shirt, jeans, flip-flops, and a ball cap. The ball cap was a gift from his sister, and he wore it with pride. It said "Purple Heart" and had a military insignia that shows that he fought in Vietnam. Rick may not have looked very hospice-like, but that was why he was there. He was a volunteer and was visiting with a World War II veteran.

The two men were decades apart in age and had served in very different wars, but the fact that they were both veterans gave them a shared experience, a bond. Rick visited with Joe weekly. He knew how to navigate the Veterans Administration and was instrumental in acquiring a scooter for Joe so he could get around more.

Rick volunteers for a hospice company in the local community and specifically visits veterans. Before Rick retired, he worked in hospitals, often with patients who were terminal. The combination of his work experiences, in the army and in hospital settings, prepared him to volunteer in this capacity. I'm sure that Rick was a more welcome sight than a nurse in scrubs. Now, of course, each has its place. But just because Rick didn't look typical doesn't mean that he didn't have a valuable role to play.

> And Mary said, "Behold, I am the servant of the Lord; let it
> be to me according to Your word." (Luke 1:38)

Sometimes our life experiences prepare us to be valuable to others. Our struggles can help us understand those who are struggling as we have; and our joys can help us celebrate with those who are experiencing the same kind of joy. Mary and Elizabeth celebrated similar experiences. They both had been visited by the angel Gabriel and had been told they were to have a miracle baby. There aren't many people who can share that kind of experience! After Mary was visited by Gabriel, she hurried off to visit Elizabeth and spent three months with her. Mary was likely a welcome friend to Elizabeth, who had chosen to stay secluded at home for a good portion of her pregnancy. On top of that, the only person there was not talking to her. Her husband, Zechariah, had been prevented from talking by the angel Gabriel. Elizabeth probably really appreciated the company. Also, we can assume that Elizabeth was a wonderful support to Mary since she was about six months behind Elizabeth in the pregnancy journey. Although it doesn't say so in the Bible, if we do the math, we can guess that Mary was probably there for the birth of John. We can surmise that Elizabeth helped to educate Mary in what was to come. They could support each other in their unique, exciting, yet scary adventure.

1. Read Luke 1:24–45. What did Elizabeth do when she found out she was with child? How did Mary find out Elizabeth was pregnant? What limited Elizabeth's husband, Zechariah, in being an encouragement to her? What story do these verses tell us?

2. What was Elizabeth's reaction to Mary's visit?

3. What did Elizabeth say to Mary that was encouraging to her?

4. Read 2 Corinthians 1:3–7. According to verse 4, what is the reason that God comforts us?

5. Write Romans 12:15 in the space below. How can you apply that to your life?

Journal Prompt

People who have gone through something tough are sometimes the ones who are best equipped to help others go through a similar tough thing. Support groups are made up of people who struggle with the same issue. Twelve-step programs are run by people who have found victory over a particular addiction. At times, all we need is someone who can listen and understand; and who understands better than someone who has walked that walk? For your journal today, write a prayer asking God if there is someone you can come alongside to offer a listening ear or understanding heart. Think of ways you could get involved in something you know well, have struggled with, or have a passion for.

Called to Give an Answer for the Hope That You Have

Not all of our ministry is something that we seek, plan, and execute. Sometimes we witness to others most strongly while we are dealing with the stuff of life. When life gets tough, people see what we are made of. They see what is really inside us and who we really lean on. This might be when people can see Jesus in us most clearly. This week, instead of looking for areas where we can serve, we will consider how we can make the most of unexpected opportunities to show people Jesus living in us.

Memory Verse: "But in your hearts honor Christ the Lord as holy, always being prepared to make a defense to anyone who asks you for a reason for the hope that is in you; yet do it with gentleness and respect." 1 Peter 3:15

DAY 1

BREAKFAST CLUB

Read 1 Samuel 18:1–5; 20:1–42.

As I loaded two of my three kids into the car, I was feeling guilty. *I should be doing something productive instead of going off to play.* A deadline loomed for a book I was supposed to be writing. There was always something to do around the house. Instead, I was off to have breakfast with some of the other preschool moms. Monthly, on a day when our children were in school, we met at someone's house to share breakfast and visit while our younger children played.

After getting everyone buckled in, I started the car, put it in drive, and started off. "God," I prayed silently, "I know I should be doing other things. I'm wasting my time. This is just frivolous. I don't need to be going to breakfast. I don't need more friends. I have plenty of friends.

"Those ladies don't need me. They have it all together. I would be doing something productive if I was actually witnessing to them or talking about You, but I'm not. I barely say anything." I went to the breakfast, still feeling guilty about going, and now also feeling self-imposed pressure to witness my faith.

It was at one of these gatherings that Carolyn referred to me as a nun. *A nun? What did she mean by that? I'm not Catholic. And I'm married!* I decided it was her artless way of saying that she saw that I had a relationship with God. Even though she said it in a condescending way, it was truly a compliment. Despite the fact that I felt like I wasn't being much of an ambassador for Jesus, He was still shining through.

A few months later, Theresa called me. "Beth's brother committed suicide last night."

I sucked in my breath; I didn't know what to say. Theresa continued, "Beth went up north to be with her parents." Then she told me that when she had gone through a tough time, someone had written out a list of Bible verses to help her through the difficulty. She asked if I would do that for Beth. Of course, I agreed.

I sat down with my Bible and searched for Scriptures that I thought might speak to Beth. I looked for words that told her of God's love for her and His promises to her and her family. And I prayed for all of them.

I had been thinking that I was simply having fun, enjoying breakfast with friends, and letting our little ones play together. I thought it was all for me, that I wasn't actively doing anything to minister to anyone else during these breakfasts. But when we have God in us, He uses everything for His glory. Though initially I did nothing but be a friend to these other ladies, I got to see how God was using that time to bring Him and His Word into their lives.

> For we are His workmanship, created in Christ Jesus for
> good works, which God prepared beforehand, that we
> should walk in them. (Ephesians 2:10)

The Scripture reading for today tells us about two unlikely friends. In 1 Samuel 18:1 we read that "the soul of Jonathan was knit to the soul of David, and Jonathan loved him as his own soul."

Jonathan, the king's son and heir to the throne, became friends with a servant boy. David was a shepherd. He came to live in the king's house because he played beautiful music that soothed King Saul when he was disturbed. It wasn't practical for the prince to strike up a friendship with a servant, but they were friends just the same. And it soon became apparent that David would be the next king and not Jonathan. King Saul was extremely jealous of David, but it didn't seem to bother Jonathan.

In fact, Jonathan asked David to be kind to him and his family when he became king. And Jonathan was able to warn David of Saul's murderous intentions before it was too late.

Sometimes we are ministering to people without even realizing it. By being who we are and living our lives as children of God, we are examples of Christ's love. And people notice.

1. Read Matthew 5:13–16. What is the context of this passage? To whom is Jesus speaking here? What does Jesus tell the people they are?

2. In John 8:12, who does Jesus say is the light of the world? What else does He say about the light of the world here?

3. How do we reconcile these two passages? Who is the light of the world? See also Luke 16:8.

4. If we have that light in us, it shines. We can't hide it. People notice it, like a city on a hill. What is the result of letting our light shine? See Matthew 5:16.

5. What are you doing that brings light to a dark world? Look for those areas in your life where you are close to people who are far from God. Even if you aren't overtly witnessing, are you letting Christ's light shine through your life? List ways you might be a light that points them to Christ.

Journal Prompt

Write a prayer asking God to show you what He wants you to do with your time. Use the items you listed above as starting points. Be general and be specific. Ask Him, "What do You want me to do?" but also ask, "Do You want me to go to these breakfasts?" "Do You want me to write a book?" His answers may surprise you.

AMBULANCE RIDE

Read Acts 16:16–40.

Steven sat in the mangled car feeling numb. The car had rolled twice and came to rest on its wheels in the median between the northbound and southbound lanes of Interstate 5. It was now just a twisted mess of metal. The helicopter airlifting his girlfriend to a nearby hospital had just left. He had tried to get on the helicopter too, but the emergency workers wouldn't even let him get out of the car. His injuries weren't as severe, so there was no reason to airlift him. He was worried about Shea. Although she had awakened just before the helicopter took off, it was because she had blacked out and then had a seizure that they felt it necessary to airlift her in the first place.

Shortly after the ambulance arrived, an EMT was at Steven's door with a gurney. "I can get myself in the ambulance." Steven started to climb out of the car.

"No," the EMT said, stopping him. "We need to help you."

Steven resigned himself to letting them take care of him. They wheeled him over to the ambulance and through the back door. The interior of the ambulance reminded him of a doctor's office with all of the medical supplies and instruments you might want. He was lying on the gurney with two EMTs sitting beside him.

As one of the EMTs put a blood pressure cuff around Steven's arm, she told him, "The helicopter with your girlfriend on it has already arrived at the hospital." That was good news, but he wondered again if she was all right. He silently said yet another prayer that she would be completely well.

He realized that except for when he was praying, he had been talking to the EMTs since they arrived.

"It's about a forty-minute drive to the hospital," the woman commented.

"Wow, well I guess so. We are quite a ways outside of town."

The other EMT glanced out the back window and said, "We didn't expect to find any survivors. We haven't seen many cars that look like that that anyone lives through."

That was a sobering thought, and again Steven wondered how Shea was doing. He thought, *I don't want to know what life is like without this woman. If she makes it through this, I'm going to ask to marry her.* He followed this up with a silent prayer: *Please God, don't take her.*

Then he remembered the EMTs sitting next to him. He thought about what the man had just said, that they shouldn't have lived through that wreck. "Well, that was all God's doing. Do you believe in God? 'Cause you should. He saved us today," Steven said.

We have a forty-minute drive and these two can't go anywhere, Steven told himself. *I have a captive audience. I can witness to them.* So Steven talked about how God had saved them, that day and for all eternity. There wasn't any forethought or plan in what Steven said. He just said whatever popped into his brain.

When they finally got to the hospital, the EMTs might have been relieved to leave Steven at the ER and not have to listen to his constant babbling. At the same time, there is no telling what Steven might have said that God used to penetrate their hearts.

> Lord, be our light when worldly darkness veils us;
> Lord, be our shield when earthly armor fails us;
> And in the day when hell itself assails us,
> Grant us Your peace, Lord. (*LSB* 659:3)

Paul and Silas also were in a very undesirable situation. After being beaten, they were chained and locked in prison. They spent their time there singing praise to God. Their prison guard couldn't go anywhere. He had to stay and hear them sing. Then, when the earthquake opened up the way for them to leave, they chose to stay, using the opportunity to minister to the prison guard. Steven, Paul, and Silas, all three, would have preferred to be somewhere else, but this was where they were, so they decided to make the most of it. In doing so, they were able to share the Gospel. They simply spoke it and let God handle bringing it home.

We probably will never see how God used Steven's testimony, but we got to see the results of Paul and Silas's witness.

1. What happened to Paul and Silas in Acts 16:22–24?

2. What did Paul and Silas do in verse 25? What are your thoughts about the contrast between the previous verses and this one?

3. Reread the memory verse for this week, 1 Peter 3:15, and Colossians 4:5–6. What do these passages tell us to do in our dealings with others?

4. Contrast those verses with Mark 13:11. How does this verse seem to be saying something opposite from the first two?

5. How does Colossians 3:16 reconcile these two concepts?

An interesting thing about Colossians 3:16 as a Scripture passage for this story is that singing is exactly what Paul and Silas were doing. God dwelt in them richly and even though they were in chains, they were singing and then had the opportunity to teach a bit later.

Steven also let the word of Christ dwell in him richly. He was raised in a Christian home and went to Christian schools. At the time of the accident, he and his girlfriend, Shea, were on their way back to their Christian university. Now, Steven and Shea are married, and Steven is the worship leader at their church. He leads the singing regularly. And he still opens his mouth and lets whatever come out.

6. We are told to be ready to give an answer for the hope that we have. What hope do we have? See 1 Peter 1:3–5.

Journal Prompt

Recall a time when things looked pretty bleak for you, but in hindsight, you see how God was right there in the situation, providing for you and protecting you. Were you able to give an answer for the hope that you have?

DAY 3

A LIVING SACRIFICE

Read Job 1–2.

Note: Today's reading sets the stage. The next several chapters tell about Job's "friends" accusing him of wrongdoing and Job asserting his innocence. Jump back to chapter 19 to see one of the responses Job makes to his friends.

"I will give you a few minutes to talk," the doctor said as he left the exam room.

Bob looked at his wife, Tennie, and for a moment, he said nothing. There was a lot to process. He had a rare form of leukemia, a type of cancer that required months of hospitalization. As they talked about what this meant, they agreed that this disease wouldn't take Bob's life. But it was something he would have to walk through. They decided that there had to be a higher purpose for all of this.

"Let's pray." Bob took Tennie's hands in his and bowed his head. He began by praising God who has all things in His hands. He thanked God for bringing this cancer to light so incredibly early, giving them an even better chance at defeating it. He prayed for himself, his family, friends, and the doctors. He concluded, "Lord, maybe someone's heart can be changed or maybe even someone's eternity because of what we have to walk through. Help us to look for opportunities to minister through this." Bob's prayer of asking God for help was actually a prayer of offering himself as a living sacrifice. He was open to what God would do through him as he dealt with this illness and the drastic treatment.

Bob didn't have to wait long. He checked into the hospital the very night he got the diagnosis. Tests began immediately and within a few days he was on twenty-four-hour chemo. He had a few days before the effects of the chemo started ravaging his body. He was brought to death's door, but it was apparent to all who attended him that he looked to God for strength and healing and to make it through another day. Bob and Tennie's prayers, their attitude, their love were all a testimony to the God who was right there with them through everything.

One particular day, Bob was struggling to deal with diarrhea, a side effect of the treatments. He was scheduled for tests in radiology that would take some time to perform. He prayed that he would last through the tests without incident. Bob talked to the tech who was attending him in radiology and learned that this man had struggles in his own life. His mother and brother had died within the year and now he had medical concerns of his own.

After talking for a bit, Bob asked the tech, "Can I pray with you?" And there together, one man standing and the other lying on a gurney, the two bowed their heads and asked God to wrap His arms around the tech and his family and give them peace.

There were plenty of other opportunities for Bob and Tennie to pray with and for people during his eight-week hospital stay. The Bible verse that their daughter artistically drew was hung on a wall and provided conversation starters. Bob prayed at the outset of this illness that God would use the illness and his witness so others might see God's mercy— and God did just that.

> Rejoice always, pray without ceasing, give thanks in all
> circumstances; for this is the will of God in Christ Jesus for
> you. (1 Thessalonians 5:16–18)

In our Bible reading today, Job was afflicted. First, he lost all his possessions and his children, and then he was covered with sores from head to foot. Life was looking pretty bleak for Job. In fact, one of the first things Job did was curse the day he was born. But when his wife told him to "curse God and die" (Job 2:9), Job refused. In Job 19:25–26, in the midst of his suffering, Job utters some prophetic words of praise: "For I know that my Redeemer lives, and at the last He will stand upon the earth. And after my skin has been thus destroyed, yet in my flesh I shall see God." Even through loss and illness, Job praised God.

It is easy to praise God when things are going well. But when the rug is pulled out from under you, what is important to you is revealed. Then people can see if you really put your trust in God. Then you have an opportunity to witness like none other. Romans 12:12 says, "Rejoice in hope, be patient in tribulation, be constant in prayer." That verse captures Bob's attitude about his leukemia. This verse is one we all can apply to our own lives, even without the drastic diagnosis.

1. Read Romans 12:1. What does "living sacrifice" mean? Bob's story is one example, but we don't have to limit ourselves to illness. What are other examples of a living sacrifice?

2. Read Romans 12:2. If we are going to be living sacrifices, how do we go about doing that? What mind-set do we need?

3. Read 1 Corinthians 6:19–20. We can think of verse 19 in terms of taking care of our bodies: eating right, exercising, that sort of thing. But verse 20 goes further. How can our bodies be temples for the Holy Spirit?

4. Job lived before Jesus and before there was any talk of our bodies being temples of the Holy Spirit. But even so, how was Job a living sacrifice and his body a temple of the Holy Spirit?

5. The words of 1 Peter 2:5 provide a wonderful visual. What are we, what can we become, and for what purpose?

Journal Prompt

It is not easy to praise God when everything seems to go wrong. (It can be hard to praise Him when just one thing goes against the way we want it to go.) But if our bodies are temples of the Holy Spirit and we are living sacrifices, then even when we are not happy with our circumstances, we can glorify and praise God. We know that our Redeemer lives and, in the end, we will see Him face-to-face. Consider your own life and your circumstances. Choose one thing you would rather not have as part of your life. Start your journal entry by writing out Romans 12:12. Then write about that one thing and explore how God can be glorified through it. By embracing this problem, you offer yourself as a living sacrifice. Conclude your journal entry by addressing how you can rejoice in hope, be patient in tribulation, and be constant in prayer.

DAY 4

BLOGGER

Read Psalm 102.

It was well after midnight when Tennie sat down with her laptop. It was quiet now. She was physically and emotionally tired and just wanted to lie down and go to sleep, but she hadn't blogged yesterday, and so much had happened in the last two days. The time she spent writing the blog post would give her a chance to process it all. She looked over at her husband, Bob. She sighed; finally he was sleeping peacefully. The steady beeping of the monitors had long since quit annoying her.

Tennie started typing and detailing all the developments over the last two days. Bob had been on chemotherapy for over a week; now that beast had reared its ugly head and Bob was experiencing the gruesome side effects of treatment. After typing almost nonstop for quite some time, Tennie stopped and read over what she had written. *Whew,* she thought, *there's a lot of technical stuff here.* But it was cathartic to write it all down. She continued writing: "Though there were frightening moments in these last few days, always we feel the strength of Christ guiding us. The peace both Bob and I have amazes me even as I experience it." One of the things she had realized during their journey with cancer was that God doesn't change. Just because their circumstances had changed, God had not. She felt comfortable telling God all her fears, doubts, and frustrations. And she knew He heard her, loved her, and was taking care of her.

As a friend of Tennie and Bob's, I read her blogs regularly. Often, they started with the down-and-dirty of the circumstances, but they would come around to praising Jesus by the end. Tennie wrote about everything she was thinking, the frustration, fear, doubt . . . and the faith. You couldn't be a regular reader of Tennie's blog and not notice all the hope and trust and faith she had in her Lord. Tennie might have used the blog to decompress, but whether or not she intended to, she also used it to witness about her faith in God.

This is a common structure of the psalms as well. David often wrote like this. He laid his complaints before his God, but by the end of the psalm, he was remembering how faithful God had been in the past, how powerful God was, and how much He loved His people. It is unclear who wrote the psalm we read today, but it follows this same format. This stems from an attitude that no matter the life circumstances we find ourselves in, God is faithful and good. When we understand that deeply, it shines even if everything else looks bleak.

1. Read 2 Corinthians 4:13–18. What gives us the ability to praise God even when it looks like everything has gone wrong?

Look to these psalms as you answer the next three questions: 3, 13, 31, 52, 64, and 102.

2. Find the transition word or words that move the psalmist from his lament into praise and write them here:

3. Write some (not all) of the complaints you see at the beginning of the prayer. Which do you particularly identify with?

4. List some of the phrases that praise God in these laments.

Does your faith show through in your answers? Do you let your light shine? Can you praise God even when the circumstances aren't desirable? It is not easy, but remembering what Jesus went through for us can make all the difference. Not everyone keeps a blog. But there may be other opportunities for you to let your faith shine through your writing: greeting cards, Christmas letters, emails, social media posts. And this doesn't have to be limited to the written word. Let your light shine through your interactions with people.

5. Read Colossians 4:6. How else can we minister to others through our choice of words?

Journal Prompt

Write a lament in the form of a prayer. Tell God something that is bothering you, difficult for you, or that you are afraid of. Lay it all out for Him. Don't hold back. Then when you have put your complaints before God, use "but" and then praise Him. Praise Him from your heart; recall times You have seen Him work in your life, or borrow phrases from the psalmists. End your lament with praise of your almighty, powerful, loving God.

HAYLEY

Read 1 Kings 18:20–19:18.

Susan lay propped up in the hospital bed with the television remote control in her hand, just flipping through the stations. Her husband, her parents, and her in-laws were all in the room—but no one spoke. No one knew what to say. It all had been said, and Susan wasn't going to hear any of it.

The phone rang and her husband, Dave, picked it up. "Pastor is on the phone. He wants to talk to you."

"Nope." Susan didn't even look away from the television, even though she wasn't seeing anything on the screen. "I'm not talking to him."

Dave held the phone up to her ear. "You don't have to talk to him, but he wants to talk to you."

Susan didn't pull away. She heard the pastor's voice over the phone line. His words were compassionate but firm. "I'm coming see you. I'm going to baptize your baby."

"You don't need to do that." Susan was angry. The pain was too much to bear. Once he baptized Hayley, the doctors were going to want to pull the plug. If he didn't baptize her, if Susan didn't hold her, if they didn't turn off the machines, then Hayley could go on living.

Susan was numb—physically, emotionally, spiritually. When it became clear that the medical professionals didn't expect her newborn to live, she fell apart. She screamed at the nurses, at God, at the empty halls of the hospital. "My voice is *not* going to be the one telling you to pull the plug!" she screamed as her husband pushed her in a wheelchair out of the NICU. She had no hope. She felt like this was what hell was like.

When the pastor arrived, everyone went back to NICU. There in that room, with all the incubators and tubes, Susan felt a peace she did not expect and could not explain. The hell she had felt before was replaced by the words of Scripture, assuring her that God is merciful and compassionate. As she held Hayley in her arms, she knew that God had her baby in His hands as well.

After the pastor baptized Hayley in the name of the Father, the Son, and the Holy Spirit, it was Susan's voice that said, "It's okay. You can disconnect her now." Susan stood to comfort her husband, who was also grieving the impending death of his child. Her faith in God gave her the strength to do what she could not do on her own. Susan and Dave were fulfilling their vocation as parents by having Hayley baptized. And they have the comfort that only Baptism can give.

Elijah's story is very different from Susan's, but there are similarities too. They were both worn out physically. They both had lost all hope. And they both had God to sustain them, work through them, and give them strength when they had none of their own. God told them both to continue on, and He gave them what they needed when they needed it.

Sometimes we don't have the strength to be there for anyone else. Sometimes we don't have the strength to reach out. But in our brokenness, God fills the emptiness. And in that moment, those around can see that only by the grace of God can we keep on going to touch another soul.

I was in church the morning this happened. Pastor left the hospital and came straight to church. He scrapped the sermon he had prepared and instead preached about his experience in the hospital. He didn't talk about the absolute despair of these parents. He spoke about their tremendous faith as they made the decision to disconnect the machines and let go of their baby girl, knowing that as a baptized child of God, she would live eternally with Jesus.

1. Read Ephesians 3:17–18. What could have happened in Susan's life that prepared her for this?

2. Read Romans 5:6–8. Describe the love of Christ for us.

3. Read Ephesians 3:14–16; James 1:5; and James 4:8a. How can we become rooted and established in love?

4. Read Zechariah 4:6 and 1 Corinthians 2:3–5. Was it Susan's strong faith and knowledge of God that made this such a powerful witness? Explain.

5. Look up Romans 15:13 and write it in the space below.

6. Read 1 Thessalonians 5:23–24. Susan was a conduit for God's promise, joy, and peace to all those around her. Through her faithful witness, those around were able to experience that joy and peace also. Where do we get the ability to take on things bigger than us, like having peace and joy as we say good-bye to our loved ones? What characteristic of the One who called you are you reminded of?

Journal Prompt

In this session, we have explored how God provides for and protects His beloved children. Now think of a time in your own life, or in the life of someone close to you, when the Lord's faithfulness and provision were evident. How was His mercy manifested? Who wore the mask of God in that situation? Write a prayer praising God for His faithfulness, commending all cares to Him, and seeking His peace.

Conclusion

HOW HAS GOD CALLED YOU?

John 13:34–35

> "A new commandment I give to you, that you love one
> another: just as I have loved you, you also are to love
> one another. By this all people will know that you are My
> disciples, if you have love for one another."

Jesus said this to His disciples just before He was arrested, tortured, and crucified for them and us. We have spent eight weeks looking at how God has used and is using His people as masks to show His love to others.

You are not expected to do everything in this book. God calls different people to different ministries. Look back over your journal entries. What are you already doing? What new areas is God calling you to?

For your final journal entry, write a prayer asking God how He wants to use you. Also ask for God's power to respond to His call.

We conclude this study with this passage:

I do not cease to give thanks for you, remembering you in my prayers, that the God of our Lord Jesus Christ, the Father of glory, may give you the Spirit of wisdom and of revelation in the knowledge of Him, having the eyes of your hearts enlightened, that you may know what is the hope to which He has called you, what are the riches of His glorious inheritance in the saints, and what is the immeasurable greatness of His power toward us who believe, according to the working of His great might that He worked in Christ when He raised Him from the dead and seated Him at His right hand in the heavenly places, far above all rule and authority and power and dominion, and above every name that is named, not only in this age but also in the one to come. And He put all things under His feet and gave Him as head over all things to the church, which is His body, the fullness of Him who fills all in all. (Ephesians 1:16–23)

Leader Guide

WEEK 1 — Day 1

Read the following verses and identify David's vocation and whom he serves.

1 Samuel 16:21: Armor-bearer; he mainly serves the king, but also other soldiers.

1 Samuel 16:23: Musician; in this case he was again serving the king, but also all those who heard his music.

1 Samuel 17:12: Son; he loves and serves his father and presumably, though not mentioned, his mother.

1 Samuel 17:17–18: Brother; his brothers (and sisters) and their commander.

1 Samuel 17:34–35: Shepherd; his family, those who would benefit from the wool and meat.

1 Samuel 17:50: Giant slayer; the soldiers and all the people of Israel.

1 Samuel 18:1: Friend; Jonathan.

1 Samuel 18:5: Warrior; the king, the other soldiers, and the people of Israel.

1 Samuel 25:40: Husband; his wives; in this case Abigail is mentioned, but David had many wives.

2 Samuel 5:14: Father; his children.

2 Samuel 6:14–15: Worship leader; all those who were celebrating with him.

2 Samuel 7:29 (all of chapter 7 would be good to read): Servant of God or child of God; all who witnessed his relationship with God, including us.

2 Samuel 9: Benefactor; Mephibosheth.

1 Chronicles 11:1–3: King; his subjects.

1 Chronicles 22:1–5: Building planner; Solomon, the people of Israel, and many more people for generations to come.

Psalm 8: Psalm writer; all who read his psalms, including us.

1. *In the Lord's Prayer, we pray, "Give us this day our daily bread" (Matthew 6:11). List as many vocations as you can that God utilizes to answer this prayer. Start with the farmer who grows the grain.* The farmer who grows the grain, the workers who harvest it, the miller who grinds the grain, the wholesaler who brings the grain to the baker, the baker who bakes the grain into bread, the distributors, the merchant who sells the bread.

2. *Let's talk about our vocations. What is the second-greatest commandment, according to Mark 12:31?* "You shall love your neighbor as yourself." *How does this passage support the doctrine of vocation?* Vocation is our calling to love and serve our neighbor. In the preceding verse, Jesus tells us that the greatest commandment is to love God "with all your heart and with all your soul and with all your mind and with all your strength." After that, we should love our neighbor. It seems pretty important to God.

3. *As children of God, we know that we have been redeemed, saved by Jesus. He paid for every one of our sins on the cross. We can't do anything more to save ourselves. We can't improve on what God has already done for us. How does Galatians 5:14 speak to this?* We are free from sin and death because Jesus has secured that freedom for us. *What are we to do in response?* We don't have to do anything to earn our salvation. We *can't* do anything to earn our salvation. What we *can* do as we enjoy the freedom that Jesus provided for us is to love our neighbor.

4. *Who is your neighbor? Read Luke 10:25–37.* Anyone you come across who is in need.

WEEK 1 — Day 2

1. *Read Exodus 3:13–22. Who is going to bring the Israelites up out of the affliction of Egypt?* The Lord, the God of Abraham, of Isaac, and of Jacob, would deliver them from Pharaoh's oppression. *Who was the mask?* Moses was God's mask.

2. *Read Exodus 4:13–17. How do these verses illustrate the mask concept?* God tells Moses to speak to the people for Him. God was going to lead the people out of Egypt, and He would use Moses as His mask to give the people directions and tell them what they were to do.

3. *According to 1 Corinthians 12:4–7, what does Paul say about who is working through us?* God.

4. *According to 1 Corinthians 12:7, what is each of us given? Why?* The manifestation of the Spirit, for the common good. *What does that mean to you?* That means that the Spirit of God is working through us, that He is embodied in us and is working to serve our neighbors.

5. *Paul talks about our different gifts. No one has all of them; no one is called to do everything. What does 1 Corinthians 12:11 say?* "All these [gifts] are empowered by one and the same Spirit, who apportions to each one individually as He wills." *How does that apply to our discussion?* We have different gifts, different abilities, different vocations, and it is God working through us and enabling us to do the things He has for us to do.

6. *Read 1 Corinthians 10:31; Colossians 3:17; and Colossians 3:23–24. What do these verses say about our mundane or ordinary lives?* Whatever we do, we are to do it for the glory of God.

WEEK 1 — Day 3

1. *Read Esther 2:5–8. What do we know about Esther at the time she received her "call"?* Her name was Esther. She was an orphan being raised by her cousin Mordecai. They were Hebrews living in Susa, which is a major city in Persia. Their ancestors had been exiled and carried off by the Babylonians. Esther was very beautiful. The king of Persia decided he wanted a new queen, and so young virgins were taken into the harem. Esther was one of these.

2. *How do you think you would have felt or how might you have reacted if you had been Esther?* Answers will vary.

3. *Read Esther 2:8–18. Regardless of how she felt about her position, what do we know about how she handled the initial change of career?* Esther won the favor of Hegai, the eunuch in charge of the women (v. 9); in fact, she was winning favor in the eyes of all who saw her (v. 15), and eventually she won the favor of the king himself (v. 17). She followed Mordecai's instructions (v. 10) and she listened to Hegai's recommendations (v. 15).

4. *Read Esther 8:1–8. Most of what we have discussed has been Esther's call. But what was she called to do?* Esther went to the king and begged him to save her people from destruction. *Once God had her in place as the queen of Persia, what did she accomplish?* The king gave Esther and Mordecai authority to respond to the plot against the Jews. As a result, the lives of many Jews were saved.

5. *List the ways you think God has called you. This can be as big and dramatic as being queen of a vast empire so you can ask the king to save a whole race of people, or it can be as ordinary as loving a child. (I have a feeling that most of us have significantly more ordinary callings. But those are wonderful.)* Answers will vary.

6. *Read Acts 1:8. Where does Jesus say that the disciples will be His witnesses?* "Jerusalem and in all Judea and Samaria, and to the end of the earth." *Read Acts 1:4. Where are the disciples when Jesus says this to them?* Jerusalem.

WEEK 1 — Day 4

1. *Read Mark 5:1–5 and Luke 8:27–29. Describe in detail the man who met Jesus.* The man with the unclean spirit lived among the tombs. He roamed around naked, and no chains could hold him because he would break them. He was crying and cutting himself with stones. Many times, he was seized by the demons and driven into the desert.

2. *What do you think this man's life had been like before this meeting?* The man must have been tormented and out of his mind. He was alone and miserable. He had not just one demon but a legion of demons living in him.

3. *Read Mark 5:6–15. What did Jesus do for the man?* He cast the demons out of the man. And when people came, they found the formerly possessed man clothed and in his right mind.

4. *In Mark 5:18, what was his response to Jesus?* He begged to go with Jesus.

5. *Write what Jesus said to the man in Mark 5:19.* "Go home to your friends and tell them how much the Lord has done for you, and how He has had mercy on you."

6. *What has the Lord done for you? How has He had mercy on you? Brainstorm and list things God has done for you.* Answers will vary.

WEEK 1 — Day 5

1. *Look up the following Bible verses. Fill in the chart to show why the person God called didn't seem like a good choice—either to the person being called, or to the rest of us—and then how this chosen one was able to glorify God:*

    Judges 6:11–15; 7:20–23   Luke 1:26–34; 1:46–55
    Judges 14:1–4; 16:23–30   Luke 5:1–11; 9:18–20
    1 Samuel 16:1–13; 17:46–47   Acts 9:1–16; 19:11–12
    Isaiah 6:1–5, 8

Called Servant	Unlikely Choice	Glorified God by:
Gideon	His clan was the weakest in Mannaseh, and he was the least in his family. When the angel found him, he was hiding from the Midianites in a winepress.	Leading God's army into victory against the Midianites
Samson	He had a weakness for women.	Killing many Philistines when he was alive and even more as he died
David	He was the youngest in his family and a shepherd boy.	As a boy, declaring that all would know that there is a God in Israel and that the victory belongs to God
Isaiah	He is self-proclaimed as a man of unclean lips living among people of unclean lips.	Volunteering readily when he heard God asking who to send to the people
Mary	A virgin chosen to give birth to God's Son.	After meeting with Elizabeth, singing a song glorifying God
Simon Peter	He told Jesus to go away because he knew that he was a sinful man.	Professing that Jesus was the Savior
Saul/Paul	He was tracking down Christians and having them thrown into jail. Jesus said that Saul was persecuting Him.	Performing miracles by the power of God and, elsewhere in Scripture, traveling extensively to preach Christ's Gospel and writing many letters proclaiming Jesus' salvation.

2. *Then there was Jonah. Read Jonah 1:1–3. What was his reaction to God's call?* Jonah ran away from the Lord.

3. *Read Jonah 4:1–3. Why did Jonah run away from what God wanted him to do?* Jonah knew that God was compassionate and would forgive— and he did not want the Ninevites to be forgiven.

4. *Read Jonah 3:1–5. What did Jonah accomplish by resisting God's call?* Jonah did not accomplish anything. After God got Jonah's attention, He sent him again. He still spoke to the Ninevites. They still repented, and God still did not destroy them. *What can we learn from this?* Just because we say no, God doesn't let up. He will continue to send us.

5. *In Exodus 4:10, Moses told God that he wasn't a very good speaker and so he was not the right person for the job. What limitations do you have that you think keep you from doing something?* Limitations will vary. *Do you think God can use you in spite of those limitations or even because of them? Read Philippians 4:13.* Yes, God can use me in spite of my limitations. "I can do all things through Him who strengthens me."

WEEK 2 — Day 1

1. *Fill in the blanks of this week's Bible verse, John 15:5:* "I am the **vine**; you are the branches. Whoever **abides** in Me and I in him, he it is that **bears** much fruit, for **apart** from Me you can do nothing."

2. *According to John 15:5, what empowers us to do anything?* If we abide in Him, we bear much fruit. God living in us makes us able to accomplish things, great things.

3. *Look up John 15:5 in various translations. What are some other words that are used for "abides"?* "Lives," "remains," "stays joined to," "dwelleth." *What does it mean to "abide in God"?* Abiding in God means to stay connected to God, to rely on Him and His abilities and stay close to Him.

4. *Read 2 Corinthians 3:4–6. What does this passage say about where our abilities come from?* Our abilities—our "sufficiency"—come from God.

5. *What does Galatians 6:9–10 tell us to do, and what will we gain from it?* It tells us to do good to everyone, especially other Christians, and we will reap a harvest if we do not give up.

6. *Who does 1 John 3:1 say we are?* Children of God.

WEEK 2 — Day 2
Read Acts 15:36–41.

1. *What were Paul and Barnabas planning?* Paul and Barnabas were planning a missionary journey to revisit all the places that they had been before. *What problem came up?* They had a disagreement about taking Mark with them. Barnabas wanted to take him along, but Paul did not because he had not finished the trip last time. *How was it resolved?* Paul chose to take Silas with him instead, and Barnabas went ahead and took Mark. *What was actually a silver lining about this resolution?* The exciting thing about the way this was resolved is that now there were two groups going out to minister to the new Christians rather than just one. They doubled their mission outreach.

2. *Let's back up and see what inspired this disagreement. Read Acts 13:5, 13. (Remember, we are reading about John Mark. These passages use the name John, but it is the same man.) What happens in these verses?* John Mark was assisting them in their ministry when they were in Cyprus, at the very beginning of the trip. But when they left Cyprus to go on to Perga, John Mark went the opposite direction and returned to Jerusalem.

3. *What do we learn about John Mark's relationship with Barnabas in Colossians 4:10?* Most translations say that Mark was Barnabas's cousin. But that term tends to denote a close family relation, not necessarily cousins as we know them. The King James Version says that Mark was Barnabas's sister's son, which would have made him Barnabas's nephew. The important thing here is that Mark was related to Barnabas.

4. *Look at Colossians 4:10 again and 2 Timothy 4:11. What can you glean from these two passages about Paul's feelings for Mark after the young man had had a chance to mature?* Paul basically sends a letter of recommendation to the Colossians on Mark's behalf. Then he asks Timothy to come see him in Rome. He also asks Timothy to bring Mark because he is very useful to him for ministry. It seems that at the start of the second missionary journey, Paul considered him useless, but now, when Paul is in need of companionship, Mark is one of the people he wants with him, because of his usefulness.

5. *What did Mark write that shows that he did indeed mature and was working to spread the Gospel?* He wrote the Gospel of Mark.

WEEK 2 — Day 3
Read Acts 11:19–21.

1. *What happened to the followers of Christ after Stephen was martyred?* A persecution arose that resulted in the followers of Christ being scattered.

2. *What did God do with the scattered people?* God was with these people, and they shared the story of Jesus with Jews and even some Gentiles.

3. *What was the eternal result of the people being scattered?* A great number of people turned to the Lord.

4. *Read Romans 1:8–15. What does Paul say he wants to do?* He wants to go to Rome to preach the Gospel. *Why didn't he do it?* He was prevented from doing so at this point.

5. *Paul eventually did make it to Rome. Read Acts 25:11–12. Under what circumstances was his travel arranged?* Paul was in prison, and after having testified before many people, he finally appealed to Caesar. Festus, the Roman governor, decreed that he would indeed go to Rome to make his appeal. So, in Acts 27, the Roman government made it possible for Paul to finally travel to Rome.

6. *What did God say to Paul in Acts 23:11?* "Take courage, for as you have testified to the facts about Me in Jerusalem, so you must testify also in Rome."

WEEK 2 — Day 4

Read Psalm 8.

1. *The first three verses are full of praise for God, detailing how magnificent He is. What question does the psalmist ask in verse 4?* "What is man that you are mindful of him, and the son of man that you care for him?"

2. *Even though God has set His glory in the heavens, are* you *important?* Yes. *How do you know? Verses 5–8 will help you answer this question.* Verse 5 tells us that God crowned us with glory and honor. Verse 6 tells us that God gave us dominion over the works of His hands.

3. *Read John 5:1–9. How many invalids were there at Bethesda?* There were "a multitude of invalids." *Could Jesus have healed all of them at once?* Of course Jesus could have healed all of them. *How many does the Bible record Jesus healing at that time?* The Bible only tells us that He healed one at that time.

Read Mark 5:21–34.

4. *Who comes to Jesus in verse 22 to ask for help? State his name and position.* Jairus, a ruler of the synagogue, fell at Jesus' feet, imploring Him to heal his daughter who was at the point of death. *Was he an important person?* As a ruler in the synagogue, he seems to have been an important person.

5. *Who interrupts Jesus as He is on His way to save the little girl?* A woman wanting to be healed. She had suffered a great deal and had sought healing from a discharge of blood for the past twelve years. She thought if she just touched His robe, she would be healed. She didn't intend to delay Jesus in His important errand. *Did she seem to believe that she was worthy of Jesus' time?* It did not seem like she felt worthy of Jesus' time. She didn't even approach Him until He asked who had touched Him.

6. *What did Jesus do that conveyed that He wasn't too busy for her but that she was indeed important and that He cared for her?* Jesus paused in His mission to save the daughter of an important official. He sought the woman out. He called her "Daughter" and told her that her faith had made her well. Then He said, "Go in peace, and be healed of your disease" (v. 34). Technically, by touching Him, she had made Him unclean according to Jewish law. He could have been upset about that, but He didn't even mention it.

WEEK 2 — Day 5

1. *Read Acts 7:20–22. This is Stephen's summary of the story we read earlier in Exodus. Look especially at verse 22. What value was there in Moses being raised by Pharaoh's daughter rather than his own mom?* "[He] was instructed in all the wisdom of the Egyptians, and he was mighty in his words and deeds." He got an education that would prepare him for the plans God had for him.

2. *According to Exodus 2:6, why did Pharaoh's daughter take an interest in the baby and take him to be her own? Was it so she could raise up a future leader of the Hebrew people who could lead them out of Egypt? Exodus 1:22 gives added motivation to consider.* She took pity on him, even as she recognized him as one of the doomed Hebrew boy babies. She saw a baby in need; she did not see a great and mighty man who would be an instrument used to create havoc in her country.

She probably had no intention that he would return to his people, and certainly not to lead them out of Egypt.

3. *Let's look at another woman in this story: Moses' mother. Look at Exodus 2:1–9. What actions did she take?* She bore a son and though she was supposed to kill him, she didn't. She saw that he was a fine child (or, as is mentioned in Acts, beautiful). Instead of killing him, she hid him. Then, when she couldn't hide him anymore, she made a water-proof basket for him, placed him in it, and put it in the reeds by the riverbank. She had his sister watch over him from a distance. *What benefits did she gain from her actions?* Once the baby was found by the princess and it looked like the princess wanted to keep him, his sister stepped forward and offered to find a wet nurse to care for him. So Jochebed not only got to have her son back with her for a time, but she was paid for it.

4. *Read Genesis 15:13–14. What did God tell Abram would happen centuries before Moses was born?* Abram's offspring would live in a land not their own and would be afflicted for four hundred years. But God would deliver them, and they would plunder that nation as they left.

5. *Let's look at what happened decades later, when the grown-up Moses returned to Egypt and demanded that Pharaoh let God's people go. Read Exodus 9:13–21. In verses 15–16, what does God say He could have done?* He could have put out His hand and struck Pharaoh and the Egyptians with pestilence and cut them off from the earth. *Why hadn't God done this?* He hadn't because He raised Pharaoh up to show God's power so that His name would be proclaimed in all the earth.

WEEK 3 — Day 1

1. *What did the Lord say to Gideon in Judges 6:14?* "Go in this might of yours and save Israel from the hand of Midian; do not I send you?"

2. *What qualified Gideon to lead an army? Gideon's résumé is in Judges 6:15.* Nothing qualified him. His clan was the weakest in Manasseh, and he was the weakest in his family.

3. *Read Judges 6:16. Why was Gideon a good choice for this job?* God was the one who was going to save Israel. Gideon's qualifications were irrelevant.

4. *In Judges 13:2–5, the Lord calls another judge. What were the qualifications, indicated in 16:6, of this judge whom God used to deliver Israel? And where did these qualifications come from?* Samson had superhuman strength that came from God as long as he was obedient.

5. *Read 2 Corinthians 12:9–10. What was Paul boasting about and why?* He was boasting about his weakness because Christ's power rested on him.

6. *Where did Paul's strength come from?* It came from Christ. When he was weak, then he was strong because God's power is made perfect in weakness.

WEEK 3 — Day 2

1. *What was Andrew's analysis of their resources for feeding so many people in John 6:9?* "What are they for so many?" *What was his opinion of the boy's lunch?* Andrew didn't think the small lunch was of any consequence.

2. *What did Jesus ask Philip in verse 5?* "Where shall we buy bread for these people to eat?" *And why was He asking Philip this?* He was testing Philip.

3. *Jesus put the task before the disciples and gave them a chance to con-template how to solve the problem. Since John tells us that Jesus already knew what He was going to do, why do you think He asked Philip where to get bread?* Before Jesus performed His miracle, He was demonstrating how hopeless the situation was. If the disciples had not given any thought to how to feed so many people, they would not have been nearly as impressed with the miracle.

4. *This is not the first instance of God taking a little and using it to feed many. Read 2 Kings 4:42–44. How much bread was provided to feed how many men?* There were twenty loaves of barley for a hundred men.

5. *Look back at verse 38. What was going on at that time?* There was a famine in the land.

6. *What did the man from Baal-shalishah say when Elisha told him to give the bread to the men?* "How can I set this before a hundred men?" (v. 43). *What percentage of the men did Elisha feed?* He fed 100 percent of the men—all of them. *Did they have enough to eat? How do you know?* They had enough to eat because there was food left over when they were done.

WEEK 3 — Day 3

1. *Let's get down to the nitty-gritty right away. According to Romans 3:23, have you sinned?* Yes. *How do you know?* "For all have sinned and fall short of the glory of God."

2. *Now continue reading Romans 3:24 and then turn to Romans 6:23. What do we learn here?* Even though I have sinned, even though my friends have sinned, and even though my enemies have sinned, we are *all* justified by grace through Jesus' death. He has redeemed us and it is a *free* gift.

3. *What does Jesus tell us to do in Mark 16:15?* "Go into all the world and proclaim the gospel to the whole creation."

4. *Read Ephesians 2:4–5. What is the Gospel of Jesus Christ?* These verses capture the heart of the Gospel and specifically tell us that God loves us in spite of our failures. God loves us, even if we have messed up. And because of His great mercy, He sent His Son to die for our sins so that we could live forever.

5. *Read 1 John 4:7–12 and fill in the blanks.* "Beloved, let us **love** one another, for **love** is from God, and whoever **loves** has been born of God and knows God. Anyone who does not **love** does not know God, because God is **love**. In this the **love** of God was made manifest among us, that God sent His only Son into the world, so that we might live through Him. In this is **love**, not that we have **loved** God but that He **loved** us and sent His Son to be the propitiation for our sins. Beloved, if God so **loved** us, we also ought to **love** one another. No one has ever seen God; if we **love** one another, God abides in us and His **love** is perfected in us."

WEEK 3 — Day 4

1. *Read Jeremiah 29:12. What does God say He will do when we pray to Him?* He will hear us.

2. *In John 4, what evidence is there that Jesus listened to the Samaritan woman?* He allowed her to speak, and then most of His comments were in relation to what she had said. He let her lead the conversation, and yet He still was able to tell her that He was the Messiah.

3. *Read Mark 9:17–27. What does Jesus ask the father?* "How long has this been happening to him?" *Do you think Jesus didn't know the answer to this question?* Jesus knew the answer to the question. *If not, then why would Jesus ask the question?* Jesus gave the father a chance to tell his story, his pain.

4. *Jesus gave the father a chance to tell his story. And Jesus listened. What words did the father say in Mark 9:24 that captured the wrestling he had been doing between his hopelessness and his belief that Jesus could make a difference?* "I believe; help my unbelief!" *Can you think of a time when you wrestled like this?* Most people will answer yes to the last question.

5. *Read Proverbs 25:11. What is like "apples of gold in a setting of silver"?* "A word fitly spoken."

WEEK 3 — Day 5

1. *Let's turn to the Bible passage that talks about how we are to use social media. Read Colossians 3:17. What does this verse tell us about how we should use this form of communication?* Do it in the name of the Lord Jesus, giving thanks to God the Father through Him.

2. *It is always good to read things in context. So let's back up and start at Colossians 3:12 and read through verse 17. What if everyone approached social media this way? Make a note of the things in this passage that are helpful when posting messages and sharing links.* "Put on . . . compassionate hearts, kindness, humility, meekness"; patience and love; "[bear] with one another"; forgive; "let the peace of Christ rule in your hearts"; "be thankful"; "Let the word of Christ dwell in you richly"; teach and admonish one another "in all wisdom"; sing "psalms and hymns and spiritual songs" (perhaps post links to songs); "do everything in the name of the Lord Jesus."

3. *Look up the following verses: Colossians 4:2–4; 1 Thessalonians 5:25; 2 Thessalonians 3:1–2; Philemon 22; Hebrews 13:18–19. What is Paul saying in all of these verses?* He is telling them to pray for him and those with him. Sometimes he gives specific things to pray for, but in 1 Thessalonians 5:25, he just says, "Brothers, pray for us."

4. *How can we follow Paul's example? Think of some specific ways you can use social media in your own life.* Answers will vary but may include something along these lines: I can use social media to ask for prayers for myself, my ministries, or people I know.

5. *Read Colossians 4:7–17. What does Paul say in this passage?* Paul is telling them that he is sending information about his activities and how his ministry is going. *Can you do something similar on social media?* Many people post about what they are doing on social media. It is especially inspirational when these posts are about ministries in far-off lands. *Describe an example in your own life.* Answers will vary.

WEEK 4 — Day 1

1. *As God created the world, what is the recurring theme in Genesis 1:4, 10, 12, 18, 21, 25, and 31?* God saw that His creation was good. *What is the problem in Genesis 2:18?* It was not good that man should be alone.

2. *Read Genesis 2:18–24. What was the solution to the problem presented in verse 18?* God made woman for Adam and brought her to him. *What was tried before a satisfactory solution was found?* Before God made woman, He brought every creature that He had created before Adam but there was not found a helper fit for him.

3. *Look up the following Bible verses and summarize what God says about wives.*
   Proverbs 12:4: "An excellent wife is the crown of her husband, but she who brings shame is like rottenness in his bones."

Proverbs 18:22: "He who finds a wife finds a good thing and obtains favor from the LORD."

Proverbs 19:14: "House and wealth are inherited from fathers, but a prudent wife is from the LORD."

Proverbs 31:10: "An excellent wife who can find? She is far more precious than jewels."

4. *Look up these verses and jot down what we should be careful to not become.*

Proverbs 19:13: "A wife's quarreling is a continual dripping of rain."

Proverbs 21:9: "It is better to live in a corner of the housetop than in a house shared with a quarrelsome wife."

Proverbs 27:15–16: "A continual dripping on a rainy day and a quarrelsome wife are alike; to restrain her is to restrain the wind or to grasp oil in one's right hand."

5. *We started reading in Proverbs 31 about an excellent wife. Let's read the whole passage, verses 10–31. As you read, list the specific things this excellent Hebrew wife does. Then, next to each item, jot down how this does or could translate in your life.*

Verse 11: "The heart of her husband trusts her." I am trustworthy.

Verse 12: "She does him good, not harm, all the days of her life." I am supportive and encouraging of my husband.

Verse 13: "She seeks wool and flax, and works with willing hands." I make things for my home.

Verse 14: "She is like the ships of the merchant; she brings her food from afar." I go to the grocery store to get food for my family.

Verse 15: "She rises while it is yet night and provides food for her household and portions for her maidens." I fill the lunch boxes and make sure everyone has breakfast.

Verse 16: "She considers a field and buys it; with the fruit of her hands she plants a vineyard." I have a job that brings in income.

Verse 17: "She dresses herself with strength and makes her arms strong." I stay fit.

Verse 18a: "She perceives that her merchandise is profitable." I sell our used books online.

Verse 18b: "Her lamp does not go out at night." I make sure the bills are paid.

Verse 19: "She puts her hands to the distaff, and her hands hold the spindle." I use the talents that I have.

Verse 20: "She opens her hand to the poor and reaches out her hands to the needy." I volunteer or donate to help those less fortunate.

Verse 21: "She is not afraid of snow for her household, for all her household are clothed in scarlet." I make sure that my family is well clothed.

Verse 22a: "She makes bed coverings for herself." I make sure my home is furnished.

Verse 22b: "Her clothing is fine linen and purple." I have nice clothes.

Verse 24: "She makes linen garments and sells them; she delivers sashes to the merchant." I have an Etsy account.

Verse 26: "She opens her mouth with wisdom, and the teaching of kindness is on her tongue." I teach Sunday School.

Verse 27: "She looks well to the ways of her household and does not eat the bread of idleness." I help with homework, make sure that baseball uniforms are clean before games, and see that my husband's clothes are ironed.

6. *Now read these verses and write what else the Bible says we can do in ministry to our husbands.*

   1 Corinthians 7:1–5: Sex.

   Ephesians 5:33: Respect our husbands.

   Colossians 3:18: Submit to our husbands as is fitting in the Lord.

   Colossians 3:23–24: Work heartily, as for the Lord and not for men.

   1 Timothy 3:11: Be dignified, not slanderers but sober-minded, faithful in all things.

   Titus 2:3–5: Love our husbands and children; "be self-controlled, pure, working at home, kind, and submissive" to our own husbands.

7. *The most perfect picture of marriage is of the divine Bridegroom, Christ, and His Bride, the Church, given to us in Ephesians 5:25–27. Jesus gave Himself for us, sanctified us, and washed away our sin in the water and word of Baptism. This relationship is the model for earthly marriage. Carefully read these next two passages and summarize how a wife can make an eternal difference in her husband's life.*

   1 Corinthians 7:12–16: God may use us to show our husbands the love of Christ.

   1 Peter 3:1–6: And God can do this without us even saying a word. As we saw earlier in the study, a quarrelsome wife is not a blessing. But God can use our pure and respectful conduct to win him to the Lord.

WEEK 4 — Day 2

1. *An inspiring person in the Bible appears in Exodus 2 (not the princess, but the other woman). Her "job" lasted only a few years (probably five at the most), but the effect that she had continues to this day. What did she do that made such an impact on the world?* She was the wet nurse to Pharaoh's daughter's adopted child (which, by the way, was her own biological child). Jochebed cared for and loved Moses in those early formative years. When he was grown, he remembered where he had come from and that he was a Hebrew by birth (see Exodus 2:11). Moses went on to lead his people out of Egypt and establish the nation of Israel.

2. *Despite the short amount of time that Jochebed had with her son, how was she able to make an impact on his life?* Even though Moses was raised in Pharaoh's household as the son of the princess, he remembered that he was a Hebrew. When he was grown, he went out to "his people." *See Exodus 2:11; what phrase is used twice in this verse?* The phrase "his people" is used twice here in reference to the Hebrews. *What became of her son when he was grown? See Exodus 3:9–10.* God chose Moses to deliver His people out of Egypt.

3. *Jochebed's ministry to one has gone out to billions. Identify and briefly describe two or three other people in the Bible whose ministry to one reached many more.* Answers might include Hannah, Mary, Elizabeth, the widow at Zarephath (Elijah's widow), the Shunammite woman (cared for Elisha). *Why are you drawn to these people?* Answers will vary.

4. *Another woman in the Bible had her son only until he was weaned. See 1 Samuel 1. Who was she?* Hannah. *Who was her son?* Samuel. *What became of him? (Read 1 Samuel 3:19–20.)* Hannah raised Samuel until he was weaned. Then she "lent him to the LORD" (1 Samuel 1:28). She delivered him to Eli, the priest at the temple. Samuel was a prophet of the Lord.

5. *See 1 Samuel 2:12–26. After being weaned, Samuel was left in the care of Eli. Was Eli a model parent?* No, Eli was not a model parent. *What were his sons like? (You can read what became of Eli's sons in 1 Samuel 2:27–36 and 4:11.)* His sons were out of control and blaspheming, and "he did not restrain them" (1 Samuel 3:13).

6. *What we do with our children in the few years we have them does matter. Write Proverbs 22:6 below, and then explain what it means in your life, with your children. If you don't have children, what might it mean in the lives of children to whom you are important?* "Train up a child in the way he should go; even when he is old he will not depart from it" (Proverbs 22:6). Answers will vary.

7. *Read Deuteronomy 6:4–9. What are we to teach children and how are we to teach it?* We are to teach them to "love the LORD your God with all your heart and with all your soul and with all your might" (v. 5). We are to teach them diligently. We are to teach them when we sit, walk, lie down, and rise. We are to write God's words on our doorposts and on our gates. Basically, we are to teach our children that God is first and foremost and we are to show them that by having Him prominent in every part of our lives. *How can you apply this in your life?* Answers will vary.

WEEK 4 — Day 3

1. *Was Martha totally off base? What do the following verses say about hospitality? Note what Peter says our attitude should be like.*

   Romans 12:13: "Contribute to the needs of the saints and seek to show hospitality."

   Peter 4:9: "Show hospitality to one another without grumbling."

2. *Copy Hebrews 13:2. Then read Genesis 18:1–8 and 19:1–3. Give examples of the Hebrews verse.* "Do not neglect to show hospitality to strangers, for thereby some have entertained angels unawares." First Abraham and then Lot invited strangers into their homes, fed them, and tended to their needs.

3. *Gaius was also known for hospitality. Paul mentions him in Romans 16:23, and John writes a letter to him encouraging him to continue this hospitality. Read 3 John 1–8, focusing on verses 5–8. What does John tell Gaius that shows his hospitality is a ministry opportunity?* "Therefore we ought to support people like these, that we may be fellow workers for the truth" (v. 8). *To whom is Gaius ministering?* Gaius has taken missionaries in and supported them just because they are about the business of sharing the Good News of Jesus.

4. *Look at your answers to questions 1–3. To whom are we supposed to show hospitality?* (1) One another, the saints. (2) Strangers. (3) Church workers.

5. *Jesus is coming for a visit. He will be at your front door exactly one hour from now, and He will be staying through the next meal. How will you spend the next hour? What will you serve Him, and what will you do while He is at your home? Now compare that to your answers to the same questions if the guest were a new person at your church.* Answers will vary.

WEEK 4 — Day 4

1. *Read Exodus 20:12; Leviticus 19:3; and Ephesians 6:2–3. What message is God getting across here?* God commands us to honor our father and mother.

2. *According to Deuteronomy 27:16, how strongly do you think God feels about this command?* He says, "Cursed be anyone who dishonors his father or his mother." These are pretty strong words. And it is a command, so it seems like God is very serious about this.

3. *Read 1 Timothy 5:3–4. What does Paul say about the children and grand-children of widows?* They should show godliness to their own household and make some return to their parents. "This is pleasing in the sight of God."

4. *Continue reading 1 Timothy 5:3–8. Paul has strong words about taking care of your family. What does he say about those who don't?* He says that those who don't are worse than unbelievers.

5. *James 1:27 doesn't refer directly to parents, but what can we learn in connection with today's lesson from this verse?* James tells us that pure religion involves visiting orphans and widows in their affliction. That is a bit different from the Ten Commandments and what Jesus has to say in regard to honoring your father and mother, but it is still about showing love and respect to those who need it.

6. *Read John 19:23–27. How does Jesus honor His mother in verses 25–27?* While He is dying an excruciating death, He takes a moment to provide for His mother's future care since He won't be able to do so in a physical, earthly way.

WEEK 4 — Day 5

1. *According to Proverbs 17:6, what are grandchildren?* "Grandchildren are the crown of the aged."

2. *What is another way we receive a crown? See James 1:12.* God promises a crown of life to those who love Him and remain steadfast under trial. *How might this relate to being a grandparent?* Anyone who has made it to being a grandparent has most likely faced his or her share of trials.

3. *According to Psalm 103:17, how can a grandma's faith be a blessing to her grandchildren?* "But the steadfast love of the LORD is from everlasting to everlasting on those who fear Him, and His righteousness to children's children."

4. *What do the following verses say about our prayers?*

   James 5:16: "The prayer of a righteous person has great power as it is working."

   Proverbs 15:29: God hears the prayer of the righteous.

   Psalm 145:18–19: God hears the cries of those who call on Him in truth and He saves them.

5. *Read Psalm 102. What does the psalmist say in the midst of his prayer, in verse 18?* "Let this be recorded for a generation to come, so that a people yet to be created may praise the LORD." *Even if you don't have grandchildren, how can you minister to future generations?* I can record how God has blessed me. I can take notes in my Bible that can be shared with others. I can share stories of His love and goodness. I have even seen where people have made photo albums dedicated to recording God's blessings in their lives.

WEEK 5 — Day 1
Read Matthew 10:16–20. . . .

1. *What does verse 20 tell us about the mask of God?* "For it is not you who speak, but the Spirit of your Father speaking through you."

   Read Psalm 107:1–3. Write verse 1 on a card or slip of paper that you can keep with you and look at frequently. This passage is a reminder of where we can start with our evangelizing, with a heart that rejoices in God and knows that He loves us. "Oh give thanks to the LORD, for He is good, for His steadfast love endures forever!"

2. *In verse 2, who are "the redeemed of the LORD"? See Hebrews 9:14–15.* We who accept Jesus as our Savior are "the redeemed of the LORD."

3. *What does Psalm 107:2 say that we, the redeemed of the Lord, are to do?* Say so. *And what does that mean?* We are to tell others how God has redeemed us.

4. *Read Psalm 103:1–5 List the ways God has redeemed us that are mentioned in these verses.* He forgives my iniquity (v. 3), heals all my diseases (v. 3), redeems my life from the pit (v. 4), crowns me with steadfast love and mercy (v. 4), satisfies me with good (v. 5), renews my youth like the eagle's (v. 5).

WEEK 5 — Day 2

1. *Steve prayed that God would use him. According to Romans 6:13, what are we to present our members to God as?* Instruments for righteousness. We can be tools in God's hands.

2. *Depending on your occupation, your work environment can be one of the hardest places to share the love of God. What does Romans 12:1–2 say about this?* We are "to present [our] bodies as a living sacrifice, holy and acceptable to God. . . . Do not be conformed to this world, but be transformed by the renewal of your mind, that by testing you may discern what is the will of God, what is good and acceptable and perfect."

3. *Read 1 Corinthians 6:19–20. Why are we supposed to glorify God with our bodies?* We were bought at a price.

4. *Read 1 Peter 1:18–19. What was the price paid for you?* The precious blood of Christ.

5. *To bring this idea home, write out Hebrews 9:12.* "How much more will the blood of Christ, who through the eternal Spirit offered Himself without blemish to God, purify our conscience from dead works to serve the living God."

6. *What are we enabled to do through the blood of Christ?* We can serve the living God!

WEEK 5 — Day 3

1. *John tells the story of another man who wasn't afraid to go head-to-head with the political leaders. In this case, it was the Pharisees. Read John 9. What were the Pharisees having an issue with?* They couldn't accept that Jesus had healed the blind man. They also didn't approve of Him healing on the Sabbath.

2. *The blind man, actually the former blind man, had to give his testimony over and over. The Pharisees didn't want to hear it, so they kept asking him to tell it again; presumably they thought that his message might change. How many times did he give his testimony?* He gave his testimony three times: first to the people who noticed that the former blind man could now see; then he was taken to the Pharisees. After the Pharisees questioned his parents, they summoned him back to question him again.

3. *Twice when the former blind man was being questioned, he had the opportunity to make a confession about who Jesus is. What did he say in John 9:17 and 30–33?* First he said, "He is a prophet." Then, after they questioned him, doubted him, and reviled him, he said, "Why, this is an amazing thing! You do not know where He comes from, and yet He opened my eyes. We know that God does not listen to sinners, but if anyone is a worshiper of God and does His will, God listens to him. Never since the world began has it been heard that anyone opened the eyes of a man born blind. If this man were not from God, He could do nothing."

4. *The man was not afraid to testify to the truth. His parents were more careful. What was their answer, and what was the reason for their ambiguity (vv. 20–21)?* They said that it was their son and that he had been born blind, but they didn't know how he could now see. They suggested that the Pharisees ask him since he was of age.

They avoided answering directly because they knew that the Pharisees would put out of the synagogue anyone who confessed Jesus to be the Christ.

5. *His parents were afraid of the repercussions of speaking the truth. The man probably knew also, but he told the truth anyway. What was the result of his statement, both immediately and a little later?* He was cast out by the Pharisees. Jesus found him and introduced Himself as the Son of Man. The man worshiped Jesus.

6. *Read John 8:31–32. How do we know the truth?* If we abide in Jesus and His Word, we will know the truth, and the truth will set us free.

7. *According to John 14:16–17, why did King Ahab, King Jehoshaphat, and the Pharisees not believe the truth when it was presented to them clearly?* The Spirit of truth (the Holy Spirit) did not dwell in them and they could not see the truth.

WEEK 5 — Day 4

1. *How does James 1:27 describe pure religion?* "Religion that is pure and undefiled before God the Father is this: to visit orphans and widows in their affliction, and to keep oneself unstained from the world."

Read the prayer in Ephesians 3:14–21.

2. *Write out all the blessings you find in this prayer.* Being strengthened with power through His Spirit in my inner being; Christ dwelling in my heart; being rooted and grounded in love; strength to comprehend with all the saints what is the breadth and length and height and depth of the love of Christ; knowing the love of Christ that surpasses knowledge; being filled with all the fullness of God; God doing far more abundantly than we can ask or think; power at work within us.

3. *Read 2 Samuel 9. David also reached out to an orphan. Mephibosheth was
    an adult but still benefited from the kindness of the king. Why did David
    want to show kindness to Mephibosheth? (See also 1 Samuel 20:14–15.)*
    Mephibosheth was Jonathan's son. David and Jonathan's souls were
    knit together. They were dear friends, and David had made a pact with
    Jonathan to "not cut off [David's] steadfast love from [Jonathan's]
    house forever." David was more than honoring that agreement.

4. *Twice in this chapter, Mephibosheth is described in the same way. What
    is the one description we know about Mephibosheth?* He was lame in
    both feet.

5. *See 2 Samuel 4:4. Why was Mephibosheth lame?* When Saul and Jona-
    than died, the nurse picked up five-year-old Mephibosheth and fled.
    But she dropped him and he became lame. *Why do you think the nurse
    chose this action?* She was probably running for their lives. Mephi-
    bosheth was in line for the throne. With his father and grandfather
    dead, he was vulnerable to anyone who wanted to take the throne.

6. *David was king. Mephibosheth was grandson to Saul, the former king,
    and Mica was the great-grandson of Saul. Contrast David's actions to-
    ward the royal descendants with those of Jehoram, another king of Ju-
    dah. (See 2 Chronicles 21:4.)* David showed love and compassion to
    the descendants of Saul (and more importantly, of Jonathan). He
    blessed them with land and had them eat at his table with his family.
    Jehoram recognized that his brothers were a threat to his throne and
    had them all killed as soon as he was crowned.

WEEK 5 — Day 5

1. *Read James 5:13–16. There is much to consider in this passage, but basically, we are looking at the fact that James tells us to go to God in all situations. How does he conclude this section? What is the last sentence of this passage?* "The prayer of a righteous person has great power as it is working" (v. 16). *How does that apply to what we have been talking about?* This tells us that our prayers have power, and if we offer to pray for someone, we are offering them a tremendous gift.

2. *What does Philippians 4:6 tell us about prayer?* We should not be anxious about anything, but instead, take our requests to God. *What does this say about the power of prayer?* Prayer is effective at making things happen. Instead of trying to fix things myself or just worrying about them, I should present my problems to God, expecting Him to be able to do something for me.

3. *Read 1 Timothy 2:1–4. What does Paul say is pleasing to God?* That "supplications, prayers, intercessions, and thanksgivings be made for all people, for kings and all who are in high positions, that we may lead a peaceful and quiet life, godly and dignified in every way" (vv. 1–2).

4. *What is Paul doing in 2 Thessalonians 3:1–2?* He is asking for the Thessalonians to pray for him and those with him. *What does it look like?* He asks that God would help them in their ministry. He also asks for prayers for their safety.

5. *When praying for people, we may or may not have all the details. That shouldn't stop us from praying. How is Romans 8:26–27 an encouragement to us in our prayer life?* Even if we don't have all the details or if we don't know what is best or if we are just unsure, we can just lay the situation before God and the Holy Spirit will pray for us. We also can pray for people without even knowing what is going on in their life.

6. *My favorites of Paul's prayers were when he was praying for the people he was writing to. Paul frequently wrote a prayer in his letters. Read Philippians 1:9–11. A powerful way to pray is to pray Scripture. Take this passage and use its words to turn it into a prayer for someone you are wanting to pray for.* And it is my prayer that Tony's love may abound more and more, with knowledge and all discernment, so that he may approve what is excellent, and so be pure and blameless for the day of Christ, filled with the fruit of righteousness that comes through Jesus Christ, to the glory and praise of God.

WEEK 6 – Day 1

1. *Does Acts 17:16–34 record Paul quoting the Scriptures in his address to the Athenians?* No. *If not, what does he quote?* Paul quoted Greek poets. He spoke to the Greeks about things that they knew, and he referenced writings they were familiar with. *What thoughts do you have about why this might have been more effective?* Thoughts may vary, but note that the Bible didn't have any meaning to them, and so it was not a useful tool for sharing information about Jesus and the resurrection.

2. *How can you apply this approach when speaking with non-Christians?* I shouldn't try and quote Scriptures at people who are not familiar with them and don't believe them.

3. *What object did Paul use to start his presentation and how did he use it?* They had an altar to the unknown god. Paul used this hole in their philosophies and filled it with Jesus. He told them that he knew the unknown God and that He is everything.

4. *Read 1 Corinthians 9:22 and 10:31–33. What do these passages say about bringing the Gospel to other cultures?* Paul is telling us that we need to meet people where they are and engage them at their level and with the information they already have. "I have become all things to all people, that by all means I might save some" (9:22). "So, whether you eat or drink, or whatever you do, do all to the glory of God. . . . I try to please everyone in everything I do, not seeking my own advantage, but that of many, that they may be saved" (10:31, 33). In doing so, we may have the opportunity to save some people. *How did you see these verses acted out in the story of Nick and also the story of Paul?* Just because Nick and his group went all the way to Vietnam from the United States, the people there were interested and curious. And when Nick and his classmates drank the rice wine, they were embracing the culture of the people with whom they were trying to share the Gospel. Paul spoke to the Greeks in a different way than he had been approaching the Jews. He used their culture and their curiosity to interest them in what he had to say.

5. *Though there are plenty of people around us with whom we can share the Gospel, what does Jesus say in Matthew 28:19–20?* "Go therefore and make disciples of all nations, baptizing them in the name of the Father and of the Son and of the Holy Spirit, teaching them to observe all that I have commanded you."

6. *Isaiah 6:8 can help us with our response. What does Isaiah say when God calls?* "Here I am! Send me." *What do we learn later in Isaiah 52:7?* "How beautiful upon the mountains are the feet of him who brings good news, who publishes peace, who brings good news of happiness, who publishes salvation, who says to Zion, 'Your God reigns.'" I need to be open to God's call and I can delight in the joy of bringing Good News to those who don't know it. How exciting to tell people "Your God reigns!"

WEEK 6 — Day 2

1. *What does John say in 13:3 that Jesus knew about Himself as He got up to serve the disciples by washing their feet?* "The Father had given all things into His hands, and that He had come from God and was going back to God." He knew that He was God and had power over everything.

2. *This seemed like an incredible act for Jesus, the teacher, to stoop down and wash the dirty feet of His students. But what did He do for them the next day that was even more beneath Him? Read John 19:16–18.* He was crucified. He died on a cross for those disciples and for all of us as well.

3. *Read Matthew 20:25–28. What does Jesus say we need to do to be great?* Whoever wants to be great must be a servant. *What does He say is the reason He came?* Jesus came not to be served but to serve and to give His life as a ransom for many.

4. *Read Philippians 2:1–11. What does verse 5 say about Christ Jesus?* Christ Jesus is God. *What do the following verses say He did about it?* Yet He humbled Himself and took on the role of a servant and was even obedient to the point of death. *What will come of His actions?* Jesus is highly exalted and everyone will praise His name. *What does Paul challenge us to do at the beginning of this passage?* Paul encourages us to follow Jesus' lead and be humble and look out for others.

5. *We can't do a study on loving our neighbor without reading the story of the Good Samaritan. Read Luke 10:25–37. What did Jesus say when the lawyer asked Him what he should do to inherit eternal life?* "Love the Lord your God with all your heart and with all your soul and with all your strength and with all you mind, and your neighbor as yourself" (v. 27).

6. *Jesus told a story about who our neighbor is. Based on His story, name some neighbors that you might not normally think of as neighbors.* Answers will vary.

7. *What is Jesus' definition of being a neighbor? See verses 36 and 37.* A neighbor is someone who shows mercy.

8. *What does Jesus tell the lawyer—and us—to do?* "You go, and do likewise" (v. 37).

WEEK 6 — Day 3

1. *In the lesson for today, Paul doesn't seem to be concerned about money. What was of more value to him than money?* He was most pleased that the Philippians cared about him. Their gift was an outward display of that care. But it meant more to him that they took time and money to show support for him in his ministry and his needs.

2. *How does Paul describe the gift the Philippians gave him in verse 18?* "A fragrant offering, a sacrifice acceptable and pleasing to God."

3. *What else does Paul say is a fragrant offering and a sacrifice in Ephesians 5:2?* Christ's love and giving Himself up for us.

4. *In Philippians 4:19, what blessing does Paul say will come from their sacrifice?* God would supply every need of theirs out of His riches and glory in Christ Jesus.

5. *Romans 15:22–33 is like a support letter from Paul to the Romans. He tells them what he intends to do and asks for their help in accomplishing it. He alludes to their previous financial help in the beginning and shows them how others have risen up to help those in need. But what does he ask for directly? In other words, what does he most desire from them?* Prayer. He "appeal[s]" to them to "strive together with me in your prayers to God on my behalf" (v. 30).

6. *Read 1 Timothy 5:17–18. What does Paul say in reference to what we are studying today?* Missionaries should be paid for their work. *What does the analogy of the ox mean? (Paul also quotes this law in 1 Corinthians 9:8–12.)* Just like the ox should be able to nibble some of the grain as it works, so should the worker benefit from his work. *What does Paul come right out and say in verse 18?* If we didn't get it with the word picture, Paul tells us, "The laborer deserves his wages."

WEEK 6 — Day 4

1. *According to Matthew 25:34–40, what are some things we can do for Jesus when we reach out and help "the least of these" around us?* Feed Him, give Him drink, welcome Him, clothe Him, visit Him when He is sick or in prison.

2. *Read Proverbs 19:17. What is the action verb used in this verse that shows what we are doing for the Lord when we are generous with the poor?* "Lends." *What will God do in response?* God will repay us.

3. *Think about that for a minute. How are giving to the poor and lending to God different? How are they the same?* When we give something away, we don't intend to get it or anything else back. But when we lend something, we expect to receive what we loaned back, and often with interest. In this verse, God tells us that being generous with the poor and lending to God are the same thing. *Does this verse have any impact on your attitude about giving to the poor? Is God a trustworthy credit risk?* If we take this verse to heart, we shouldn't have any trouble giving and sharing with the poor, even if our current budget is tight. God is true to His word and will repay our "loan."

4. *Read Isaiah 58:6–8. In these verses, God contrasts a traditional fast with a focus on things that matter. According to these verses, what kinds of things does God ask us to do that demonstrate our love for Him?* "Loose the bonds of wickedness," "undo the straps of the yoke," "let the oppressed go free," and "break every yoke" (v. 6); "share your bread with the hungry," "bring the homeless poor into your house," clothe the naked, and don't hide from your relatives (v. 7).

5. *What imagery is in Isaiah 58:10, and what benefit is there to honoring God's desire here?* "Pour yourself out for the hungry." If we satisfy the desire of the afflicted, then we will receive blessings from God.

6. *James is much more straightforward in his language and expectations. What is the attitude conveyed in James 2:15–16?* Saying nice things to people who are in need is not of any value. We need to actually *do* something to help them.

WEEK 6 — Day 5

1. *Read Zephaniah 3:17. The verse tells us that our mighty God is with us. What three things does it say He does?* "He will rejoice over you with gladness; He will quiet you by His love; He will exult over you with loud singing." *How does this make you feel?* Answers will vary.

2. *Read Romans 5:8 and John 15:13. After reading these carefully back-to-back, close your Bible and write the message that God is giving you here. (The first verse was penned by Paul after Jesus died. The second is words Jesus spoke before His crucifixion.)* Even though I sin and have messed up quite a bit, Jesus still loves me. He loves me so much that He willingly died for *me*. And He calls me His friend.

3. *In our Bible reading for today, Jesus talks about what a shepherd would do for his sheep and says that that is how God feels about His people. Read the following passages about our Shepherd: Psalm 23; Isaiah 40:10–11. What does Jesus do for His sheep?* Gives me what I need, pastures and water; restores my soul; leads me; is with me; comforts me; prepares a table for me; anoints my head with oil; allows me to live with Him forever; gathers me in His arms and carries me close to His heart; gently leads me.

4. *Jesus is our Good Shepherd. But sometimes He takes on a mask and asks us to tend His sheep, as He did with Peter (John 21). What does Acts 20:28 direct us to do?* Keep watch over yourselves and the flock; shepherd the Church of God.

5. *Let's return to our Bible story. In Matthew 18:5, what does Jesus say we do when we receive one of His children in His name?* We receive Him. *By showing love to one of His children, what are we doing?* We are loving Him.

6. *In Luke 12:32, what does Jesus tell us that God wants to give to His flock?* The kingdom. *What word in this verse captures the feeling of God's love for us?* Pleasure. "It is your Father's good pleasure to give you the kingdom."

WEEK 7 — Day 1

1. *Read Acts 4:19–20. When Peter and John were before the religious authorities, they were ordered not to teach or speak any more about Jesus. What was their answer?* "But Peter and John answered them, 'Whether it is right in the sight of God to listen to you rather than to God, you must judge, for we cannot but speak of what we have seen and heard.'" *How would you say that in your own words?* Answers will vary but might include something along the lines of "I have to speak what God tells me to say."

2. *After our reading, the story continues. They were released; then they went and told their friends about their experience. What did they pray for as recorded in Acts 4:29?* They prayed to be able to continue to speak God's word with boldness.

3. *Read Acts 5:17–42. What was the result of the apostles continuing to speak about Jesus?* The apostles were arrested but then freed. *What did Peter say in verse 29?* Peter said, "We must obey God rather than men."

4. *John started FUN Sports so the kids could enjoy sports in an environment where Jesus is welcome. Every week a Bible passage is shared with those in attendance. John told me sometimes he wonders if anyone really hears it. Nevertheless, he continues to share the Word of God and trust that God is faithful to work faith in the hearts of those present. Read Isaiah 55:10–11. Based on this passage, what could you say to John to encourage him to continue sharing the Bible verses?* Continue to share the Bible verses. God says that His Word will do what He sets out for it to do. You just need to read the verses and let God do the work.

5. *It was Paul's custom on the Sabbath to go to the synagogue to worship and to speak to the Jews. What does he do in Acts 16:13?* Paul and his companions went outside the city to the river, looking for a place to worship. They found some women of the city and talked with them.

What does it say God did here? "The Lord opened [Lydia's] heart to pay attention to what was said by Paul" (v. 14). Paul was speaking to the women, and God did the work and used Paul's words to help her believe in and accept Jesus. *How does this fit with the story we read about John and his FUN Sports?* This was an unconventional place to preach, just like John's soccer field is unconventional. And Paul spoke and let God do the moving, just as John shares Bible messages and relies on God to open the hearts of the people who need to hear them.

WEEK 7 — Day 2

1. *The story we read today is not the only time stones were used to commemorate an event. Read Genesis 28:10–22. What was being remembered in this passage?* Jacob had a dream in which God blessed him and promised him the blessing that He had promised to his forefathers. In the dream, Jacob saw a ladder with angels ascending and descending, and God spoke to him there. He declared that it must be the house of God and the gate of heaven. So, Jacob set up a stone there to honor God.

2. *Besides using stones to remember special events, God's people celebrated holy days in remembrance. Read Exodus 12:25–27. What holiday is instituted here?* They were celebrating Passover. *What were the children of Israel celebrating?* They were remembering when God passed over the houses of the Israelites in Egypt while striking the houses of the Egyptians. *How is this celebration observed in our worship service today?* We remember this every time we celebrate Holy Communion.

3. *What holy day was instituted in Esther 9:20–32?* Purim. *What were they celebrating?* They were celebrating the Jews being saved from destruction at the hands of Haman, who had cast a *pur* (lot) to determine the day that the Jews should be destroyed.

4. *Examples of another form of remembrance are found in these passages. What kind of remembrance was this?* Songs. *And what was being remembered in each case?*

   Exodus 15:1–18: Moses sings of God splitting the Red Sea and drowning the Egyptian troops that followed them.

   Judges 5: Deborah and Barak sing of a military victory against Sisera and Jabin.

   Numbers 21:27–30: The Israelites asked permission to pass through the region of Sihon. Not only would King Sihon not allow it, but he gathered his military to make war against the Israelites. The Israelites, under God's guidance, scored a decisive victory, seizing much territory and many cities. This song sings of their victory.

   2 Samuel 22: David sings a song of praise and thanks to God for delivering him from his enemies.

   1 Chronicles 16:8–36: When the ark of the covenant was brought to Jerusalem, David had the people sing thanksgiving to God. He included a bit of history in the song that showed what God had done for them and how He had saved them.

   Luke 1:46–55: Mary sings praise to God after she learns that she will be the mother of the Savior.

5. *What theme runs through most of these occasions of remembrance?* Most of these deal with being saved. If the people weren't being saved, then they were offering praise to God for His provision.

6. *What phrase did we come across several times in these passages?* When your children ask, "What does this mean?" *What does this suggest we should be mindful of? See Joshua 4:21; 12:26.* We can have memorials that help us share with future generations all that the Lord has done for us.

WEEK 7 — Day 3

1. *Read James 1:17. What does James say that God gives us?* Gifts. "Every good gift and every perfect gift is from above."

2. *While there are a variety of gifts from God, today we focused on material gifts such as money and possessions. Read 1 Peter 4:7–11. In verse 10, what does Peter say we should do with our gifts?* Serve one another.

3. *The last part of that verse says, "as good stewards of God's varied grace." What does that mean?* God gives different gifts to different people. We are to use well what He gives us.

4. *Why should we serve one another with the gifts that God gives us?* Verse 11b: "In order that in everything God may be glorified through Jesus Christ."

5. *What is the greatest gift God has given us?* He gave us His Son. *Why is it so wonderful?* It is so precious to us because through this gift, we are saved; we won't perish, but we will live forever with God.

6. *Read Matthew 25:14–30. What does the master say in verses 21 and 23?* "Well done, good and faithful servant. You have been faithful over a little; I will set you over much. Enter into the joy of your master." *What had these servants done to precipitate such a response?* These two servants had taken what he had given them and used it, and they gave the master back more.

WEEK 7 — Day 4

1. *Psalm 37:4 says, "Delight yourself in the LORD, and He will give you the desires of your heart." If He isn't giving what we ask for, what does that verse mean? Does that mean that we are not taking delight in Him? Or does it mean that what we ask for is not really the desire of our heart? Or will we find that God knows our heart more than we do and gives what it truly desires? What are your thoughts?* Matthew 6:33 tells us, "But seek first the kingdom of God and His righteousness, and all these things will be

added to you." These verses from the Psalms and Matthew encourage us to put God first, to seek Him, to delight in Him, and to trust Him. We can trust Him with our heart just as we can trust Him to provide for our needs. When we are fully focused on Him, we can rest in knowing that He is taking care of every little part of our lives.

2. *Read 2 Corinthians 12:7–10. What did Paul beg God for?* Paul begged God to remove the "thorn . . . in the flesh" from him. He asked for it to be removed three times. *Do you think Paul delighted in God? Did Paul get what he asked for?* Once Paul knew Jesus, he devoted his whole life to not just following Him but sharing that with others. By all outward appearances, Paul certainly seemed to delight in the Lord. And yet, Paul did not get what he asked for.

3. *What was God's response to Paul's request? Copy it from verse 9.* "My grace is sufficient for you, for My power is made perfect in weakness."

4. *How does Paul sum up this exchange with God?* "For when I am weak, then I am strong" (v. 10).

5. *What is meant by these phrases: "My power is made perfect in weakness" and "when I am weak, then I am strong"?* When I am not in control, when circumstances are too much for me, then I turn to God. When I allow God to work in my life, that is when amazing things can happen. As long as things are dependent on my strengths, there is a limit to what can happen. When I recognize that it is beyond my control and let God work in my life, that is when I am able to accomplish amazing things, because it is through His strength, not mine.

WEEK 7 — Day 5

1. *Read Luke 1:24–45. What did Elizabeth do when she found out she was with child?* Elizabeth hid herself for five months. *How did Mary find out Elizabeth was pregnant?* Mary found out that Elizabeth was pregnant from the angel Gabriel. *What limited Elizabeth's husband, Zechariah, in being an encouragement to her?* Zechariah was unable to talk from the time he found out about the baby until he was born. *What story do these verses tell us?* Elizabeth may have felt alone and needed someone who really understood.

2. *What was Elizabeth's reaction to Mary's visit?* She was delighted and honored that Mary came to visit her.

3. *What did Elizabeth say to Mary that was encouraging to her?* "Blessed are you among women, and blessed is the fruit of your womb!" (Luke 1:43). "Blessed is she who believed that there would be a fulfillment of what was spoken to her from the Lord" (v. 45).

4. *Read 2 Corinthians 1:3–7. According to verse 4, what is the reason that God comforts us?* So that we will be able to comfort those going through a similar affliction.

5. *Write Romans 12:15 in the space below. How can you apply that to your life?* "Rejoice with those who rejoice, weep with those who weep." I can come alongside others and celebrate with them in their joy and listen to them in their grief.

WEEK 8 — Day 1

1. *Read Matthew 5:13–16. What is the context of this passage?* This is from the Sermon on the Mount. *To whom is Jesus speaking here?* Jesus is talking to the crowds. *What does Jesus tell the people they are?* In His sermon, Jesus tells the people, and us, that we are the salt of the earth and light of the world.

2. *In John 8:12, who does Jesus say is the light of the world?* Jesus. *What else does He say about the light of the world here?* "Whoever follows Me will not walk in darkness, but will have the light of life."

3. *How do we reconcile these two passages? Who is the light of the world? See also Luke 16:8.* Jesus is the light of the world, and when He lives in us, then we are "sons of light" and we have that light in us.

4. *If we have that light in us, it shines. We can't hide it. People notice it, like a city on a hill. What is the result of letting our light shine? See Matthew 5:16.* Others see our good works and give glory to our Father, who is in heaven.

5. *What are you doing that brings light to a dark world? Look for those areas in your life where you are close to people who are far from God. Even if you aren't overtly witnessing, are you letting Christ's light shine through your life? List ways you might be a light that points them to Christ.* Answers and thoughts will vary.

WEEK 8 – Day 2

1. *What happened to Paul and Silas in Acts 16:22–24?* Their clothes were torn off, and they were beaten many times with rods. Then they were put in the inner jail cell and had their feet placed in the stocks. They weren't in good condition.

2. *What did Paul and Silas do in verse 25?* They were praying and singing to God while the other prisoners listened. *What are your thoughts about the contrast between the previous verses and this one?* Answers may vary, but it should be noted that they were severely beaten and treated poorly, yet they still were able to praise God and encourage the other people around them.

3. *Reread the memory verse for this week, 1 Peter 3:15, and Colossians 4:5–6. What do these passages tell us to do in our dealings with others?* Honor Christ; be prepared to share the hope you have in Christ; make the best use of your time with others; your words should be gentle, respectful, gracious, and seasoned with salt.

4. *Contrast those verses with Mark 13:11. How does this verse seem to be saying something opposite from the first two?* The first two tell us to be prepared to talk about Jesus, whereas Mark 13:11 says to not be anxious beforehand; when the time comes, the Holy Spirit will speak for us.

5. *How does Colossians 3:16 reconcile these two concepts?* It tells us to let the word of Christ dwell in us richly. With the word of Christ in us (the preparation), we can open our mouths and let the Holy Spirit speak for us.

6. *We are told to be ready to give an answer for the hope that we have. What hope do we have? See 1 Peter 1:3–5.* Through the resurrection of Jesus from the dead, we have the hope of an inheritance that is imperishable, undefiled, and unfading, kept in heaven for us. Our hope is salvation.

WEEK 8 — Day 3

1. *Read Romans 12:1. What does "living sacrifice" mean?* A living sacrifice is living our lives in service to God, being willing to set aside our own desires to be available to do God's bidding. *Bob's story is one example, but we don't have to limit ourselves to illness. What are other examples of a living sacrifice?* The ultimate living sacrifice was Jesus dying on the cross to save us from our sins so that we can live forever with Him in paradise. But in our daily lives we can offer our lives as living sacrifices.

Answers will vary but can include volunteer work, career choice, choices of activities, and choices of how to spend our time, talents, or money. Anything that we do for the glory of God can be our act of being a living sacrifice.

2. *Read Romans 12:2. If we are going to be living sacrifices, how do we go about doing that? What kind of mind-set do we need?* We need to be transformed by the renewal of our minds and seek out what the will of God is in our lives.

3. *Read 1 Corinthians 6:19–20. We can think of verse 19 in terms of taking care of our bodies: eating right, exercising, that sort of thing. But verse 20 goes further. How can our bodies be temples for the Holy Spirit?* We were bought with a price. That price is the precious blood of Jesus. Jesus redeemed us and saved us. Those bodies can be used to glorify God. We can be open and available to God working through us in our lives.

4. *Job lived before Jesus and before there was any talk of our bodies being temples of the Holy Spirit. But even so, how was Job a living sacrifice and his body a temple of the Holy Spirit?* In spite of all that Job had lost, he refused to curse God; indeed, he praised God, confessing that God was his Redeemer, and he looked forward to when he would be with God. Those around Job could see that Job looked forward to something bigger than this world.

5. *The words of 1 Peter 2:5 provide a wonderful visual. What are we, what can we become, and for what purpose?* We are living stones being built into a spiritual house to offer spiritual sacrifices.

WEEK 8 — Day 4

1. *Read 2 Corinthians 4:13–18. What gives us the ability to praise God even when it looks like everything has gone wrong?* We fix our eyes on what is unseen and eternal rather than the temporary things we can see.

Look to these psalms as you answer the next three questions: 3, 13, 31, 52, 64, and 102.

2. *Find the transition word or words that move the psalmist from his lament into praise, and write it or them here.* "But"

3. *Write some (not all) of the complaints you see at the beginning of the prayer. Which do you particularly identify with?* Answers will vary but may include: "Many are rising against me" (Psalm 3:1); "How long must I take counsel in my soul and have sorrow in my heart all the day" (13:2); "My life is spent with sorrow, and my years with sighing" (31:10); "Your tongue plots destruction, like a sharp razor, you worker of deceit" (52:2); "They hold fast to their evil purpose; they talk of laying snares secretly, thinking, 'Who can see them?'" (64:5); "My heart is struck down like grass and has withered; I forget to eat my bread. Because of my loud groaning my bones cling to my flesh" (102:4–5).

4. *List some of the phrases that praise God in these laments.* Answers will vary but may include: "But You, O Lord, are a shield about me, my glory, and the lifter of my head" (3:3); "I will sing to the Lord, because He has dealt bountifully with me" (13:6); "Oh, how abundant is Your goodness, which You have stored up for those who fear You" (31:19); "Be strong, and let your heart take courage, all you who wait for the Lord!" (31:24); "I trust in the steadfast love of God forever and ever" (52:8); "Let the righteous one rejoice in the Lord and take refuge in Him! Let all the upright in heart exult!" (64:10); "Let heaven and earth praise Him, the seas and everything that moves in them" (69:34); "Of old You laid the foundation of the earth, and the heavens are the work of Your hands. They will perish, but You will remain; they will all wear out like a garment" (102:25–26).

5. *Read Colossians 4:6. How else can we minister to others through our choice of words?* Our speech can show that we trust in God.

WEEK 8 — Day 5

1. *Read Ephesians 3:17–18. What could have happened in Susan's life that prepared her for this?* Susan was rooted and established in love and had power to grasp how wide and long and high and deep is the love of Christ.

2. *Read Romans 5:6–8. Describe the love of Christ for us.* "While we were still weak"—while we were still sinners—Christ died for us. Jesus loved us so much that He died to redeem us. That is a pretty wide and long and high and deep love.

3. *Read Ephesians 3:14–16; James 1:5; and James 4:8a. How can we become rooted and established in love?* Kneel, pray, ask God for wisdom. Draw near to God, and He will draw near to you.

4. *Read Zechariah 4:6 and 1 Corinthians 2:3–5. Was it Susan's strong faith and knowledge of God that made this such a powerful witness?* No. *Explain.* It was through her weakness; the Holy Spirit came and gave her peace and allowed her to demonstrate that peace to all those around her.

5. *Look up Romans 15:13 and write it in the space below.* "May the God of hope fill you with all joy and peace in believing, so that by the power of the Holy Spirit you may abound in hope."

6. *Read 1 Thessalonians 5:23–24. Susan was a conduit for God's promise, joy, and peace to all those around her. Through her faithful witness, those around were able to experience that joy and peace also. Where do we get the ability to take on things bigger than us, like having peace and joy as we say good-bye to our loved ones?* God. *What characteristic of the One who called you are you reminded of?* Answers may vary but should include the idea that He is faithful.